The Men with Wooden Feet

Statue of Bodega y Quadra in Victoria, B.C. Courtesy Cathie Archbould.

The Men with Wooden Feet

The Spanish Exploration of the Pacific Northwest

John Kendrick

NC Press Limited
Toronto, 1986

For Pedro

©Copyright John Kendrick 1985
Paperback edition 1986
No part of this publication may be reproduced, stored in
a retrieval system, or transmitted, in any form or by any
means, electronic, mechanical, photocopying, recording
or otherwise, without the prior written permission of NC
Press Limited.

Cover design: Doe Pon
Cover etching: Ronaldo Norden, courtesy of Galiano
Historical and Cultural Society.

Canadian Cataloguing in Publication Data
Kendrick John
    The men with wooden feet: the Spanish exploration of the
Pacific Northwest
Bibliography: p.
Includes index.
ISBN 0-920053-85-8

1. Northwest coast of North America - Discovery and
exploration - Spanish. 2. Spain - Exploring expeditions. I.
Title.
F851.5.K46 1986   970.01'6   C86-093324-5

We would like to thank the Ontario Arts Council and the
Canada Council for their assistance in the production of this
book.

New Canada Publications, a division of NC Press
Limited, Box 4010, Station A, Toronto, Ontario
M5W 1H8.

Distributed in the United States of America by
Independent Publishers Group, One Pleasant Avenue, Port
Washington, New York, 11050

Printed and bound in Canada

Contents

Maquinna, or Macuina, was the principal chief at Nootka. His hat is ornamented with whaling scenes, and has the chiefly finial on top. Courtesy Vancouver Public Library.

INTRODUCTION

The introduction to the narrative of the 1792 voyage of Galiano, who was the last of the Spanish explorers on the coast we call British Columbia, closes with these words in Latin.

Multum egerunt qui ante nos fuerunt, sed non peregrunt ...
Multum adhuc restit operis, multumque restabit: nec ulli nato
post mille saecula precludetur occasio aliquid adhuc adiicendi.
Sed etiam si omnia a veteribus inventa sunt: hoc semper novum
erit, usus et inventorum ab aliis sciencia et dispositio.

Seneca, Epist. 64

If you have no more Latin than I have, let me tell you that these words have been translated thus:

They did much who preceded us, but they did not finish it ...
Much work still remains, and much will remain: nor will
anyone born after a thousand centuries be deprived of the
opportunity of still adding something. But even if everything
had been discovered by the ancients this will always be new,
the use and the science and arrangement of things discovered
by others.

This book is an arrangement of things discovered by others, not only native tribes, animals and trees, unknown islands, bays and rivers discovered by the Spanish explorers but also records in the form of documents, drawings, maps, and artifacts discovered by historians and scientists whose works are recorded in the bibliography at the end of this volume.

The libraries and archives where I have found the records are:

Archivo General de la Nación, Mexico
British Columbia Provincial Archives, Victoria
Makah Cultural and Research Centre, Neah Bay, Washington
Museo Naval, Madrid
Public Archives of Canada, Ottawa
University of British Columbia (Special Collections),
Vancouver
University of California (Bancroft Library) Berkeley
Vancouver Public Library (Northwest History Room)

The staffs of all these institutions have been equally helpful, but I have also been helped by a number of old and new friends. My outline and work programme were assessed by two neighbours, Dr. Kaye Lamb in Vancouver and Jane Rule on Galiano Island, and by my old skipper Dr. P. R. (Dick) Sandwell. Greg Foster, the late Steve Riddell, and Dr. Morley Whillans introduced me to the Galiano story. Between them the idea of building a replica of Galiano's ship arose. That got me started. Dr. Barbara Efrat of the Provincial Museum advised me on the Indian and Latin languages. I consulted her colleague Kevin Neary and also Lynn Maranda of the Vancouver Museum on ethnology. Jane Baggott interpreted some puzzling passages in the Spanish documents. Valerie Kendrick interpreted my handwriting and converted it to a typed draft. The interest of Nancy Stuart Stubbs, Anne Yandle, and Robert Watt has been a great encouragement. At Gold River, B.C. Kim Creed, Norman Paulson, and Rene de Waal arranged the introductions for my visits to Nootka Sound and Kyuquot, while the Tahsis Company allowed me to go along on a helicopter trip to the latter place.

Photographs of pictures in the Museo Naval Español were obtained through the courtesy of the Spanish Embassy in Ottawa.

Cliff Atleo and my old friend Art Jackson of the Native Brotherhood put me in touch with the Mowachaht Band. In the text are the names of Kyuquot, Mowachaht, Makah, and Quinault people who counselled me and informed me on their history. I hope my gratitude is evident in what has been written.

Thanks also to Jean Walker for her superb editing.

Often one finds in a book an acknowledgement to the writer's spouse. Now I know why. My wife has lived with this book for a year and a half. Any writer's spouse will know what that means.

J. S. Kendrick,
Galiano Island.

1

THE EXPLORERS

At daybreak a strong southeaster was blowing and the sky threatened worse weather to come. The two little ships had anchored out in thirty fathoms the night before, to be ready for an attempt to round the point they called Cabo Scot. They had left the Spanish settlement at Nootka three months earlier and sailed south and east through the Strait of Juan de Fuca to explore the waters inside what we know as Vancouver Island. After tracing the mainland shore of the Gulf of Georgia they had worked their way through the maze of islands at its northern end, found open water, and realized they were now close to the cape.

They were anxious to get around and get back to Nootka, so in spite of the threatening weather, they made sail and ran westward before the wind; but it was not to be. They reached the cape and turned south and found themselves between the cape and the islands which lie offshore, with the wind now directly in their faces. It had veered south, as it still does when you round the cape in a southeaster, and it blew so hard they did what many a wise mariner has done since; they turned back to a safe anchorage to wait out the gale.

Four days later they made it. As this part of the coast was known to them, there was no need to explore. Again they did what many have done since — stayed out to sea until they could make out their landfall, then sailed into Nootka at daylight. It was August 31, 1792 and the little ships were the Spanish naval vessels *Sutil,* commanded by Don Dionisio Alcalá Galiano, and *Mexicana,* commanded by the junior captain Don Cayetano Valdés.

When they anchored at Nootka the Spanish exploration of the northern coast of the Californias ended. George Vancouver's ships, *Discovery* and *Chatham* had arrived four days earlier. By this margin Vancouver became the first explorer to prove that the mountain mass behind Nootka was indeed on an island. He christened it Quadra and Vancouver's Island, the former in honour of the Spanish commissioner at Nootka. The name was soon to be abbreviated to Vancouver Island, and so it remains.

Galiano did not lose the race because of the delay in rounding Cape Scott. There was no race. Vancouver was doing the same thing as Galiano; exploring and mapping the coast inside Vancouver Island. In fact, the two had met several times in the course of their voyage. They even proceeded in company at times, but the Spanish ships could not keep up with the larger English ones so they all agreed it was better to explore independently and exchange information later. This was done, and Vancouver's maps show the information obtained from "Spanish authorities," while the Spanish maps indicate the parts which were explored by Vancouver. Between them they set at rest the idea that there might be a northwest passage linking the Atlantic and Pacific, because the whole of the coast with the exception of the part shown on these maps had been explored by (among others) James Cook for the English, Quadra for the Spanish, and Vitus Bering for the Russians. Cook had actually sailed through Bering Strait and turned back only when he reached the pack ice of the Arctic Ocean.

By land, Samuel Hearne had reached the Arctic Ocean in 1771 and Alexander MacKenzie had reached it in 1789. They had come from Canada (which then did not extend beyond the Great Lakes) and if there were a northwest passage south of that ocean they would have had to cross it. This may not have been known in London or Madrid before the orders were given for the voyages, but one suspects that the captains, all experienced navigators, were not at all surprised by the negative results of their work. In fact the narrator of Galiano's voyage said their explorations served only to satisfy curiosity, without being of any profit to navigators. There were no products of sea or land worth a trader's trouble in navigating the shoal and narrow channels and there were no places suitable for settlement or even for spending the winter.

It is reasonable to presume that eighteenth century naval captains had just as low an opinion of the shore-bound high command as do their twentieth-century successors. One can imagine Galiano grumbling to Vancouver (for they were good friends and entertained each other aboard their ships) that if their respective Lords in Admiralty would forget that barroom tale of Michael Lok's they would all be saved a lot of trouble.

Lok was an Englishman who came home from Venice in 1596 and said he had there met a Greek named Apostolos Valerianos, who told him that he had served for forty years as a mariner and pilot for the Spanish. Valerianos claimed that in 1592 (two hundred years before Galiano's voyage) he had been sent to explore the Pacific Coast of North America, where he found between 47 and 48 degrees of latitude, a broad inlet wherein he sailed for twenty days through a land rich in gold, silver, and other things, finally coming out into the North Sea (as the Atlantic was then called). The Greek was using the name of Juan de Fuca. There is no evidence at all of such a voyage, and it is uncertain that Valerianos even existed, although some parts of Lok's story indicate a knowledge of events in Mexico.[1]

Perhaps Mrs. Barkley was an innocent agent in perpetuating the myth. She wrote in her diary that while she and her husband were trading on the coast in 1787 in his ship, the *Imperial Eagle,* they arrived off a large opening in latitude 48 degrees which her husband immediately recognized as the long lost Strait of Juan de Fuca.[2] Maybe Captain Barkley hadn't heard about the gold and silver, because he didn't enter. He did note it on his chart and named it after the chance acquaintance of Michael Lok.

Although Galiano and his friends underestimated the potential of the lands surrounding Puget Sound and the Gulf of Georgia we must agree with them that their voyage was not of primary importance. We would have heard little of it beyond the brief mention in Vancouver's narrative of his meetings with the Spaniards, except that, almost by accident, the narrative of Galiano's voyage was published, one of the few published accounts of a voyage by Spanish explorers to the coast of British Columbia and the only one Spain published at the time. It was published in Madrid in 1802 under the title of *Relación del Viage Hecho por las Goletas Sutil y Mexicana.*

The *Relación* or narrative, plus a mass of unpublished material in archives in Spain and Mexico, fill a gap in the history of the west coast of Canada and the United States. Perhaps that is reason enough to tell the Spanish story. However, there are other reasons. For one thing, the life and customs of the native people are described by sympathetic and respectful observers who lived beside them for several years. For another, there is a literary competence in some of the Spanish documents which is missing in many accounts of voyages to strange lands. They also have the ring of truth. We are spared the one-eyed monsters, the holes in the sea, and the mountains of gold of which we have heard more than enough.

There is one more reason. The story is *un cuento hechicero,* a rattling good yarn.

Interlude

EL SIGLO DE LA ILUSTRACIÓN

It was a turbulent time, the Age of Enlightenment. In the last half of the eighteenth century, writers such as Montesquieu and Voltaire in France, Kant in Germany, and Locke and Hume in England initiated a ferment of ideas which influenced the American Revolution in 1776 and almost certainly led to the French Revolution in 1789. The Enlightenment contained in the works of these philosophers even affected the rigid conservatism and staunch Catholicism of Spain. The *Ilustración* as the Age of Enlightenment was called in that country, not only brought philosophical enlightenment but made science acceptable, although perhaps not fashionable. Astronomy was the first science to be studied in Spain. Astronomers and hydrographers such as Galiano were, perhaps unintentionally, members of the liberal tradition which was developing in Spain in spite of fierce resistance from both secular and religious conservatives.

At the time of Galiano's voyage, Carlos IV in Madrid was perhaps less concerned with internal turbulence in Spain than with his efforts to secure the release of Louis XVI from the custody of the French National Assembly. Carlos failed, and his cousin Louis was to be executed early in 1793. This led to a two-year war against France, with England as an ally of Spain; but in 1795 a peace was concluded, followed by a war against England which lasted until the Peace of Amiens in 1802. This treaty lasted less than a year, then Spain was again at war with England.

What has all this to do with our story? During the wars, Spain was reluctant to spread word of its discoveries, or even to publish the maps that had been made. In consequence, much of the material which was the fruit of Spanish exploration was locked away in archives. Some of it was lost, and some was turned up generations later by scholars.

There was an exception. During the brief period of peace in 1802 it became known in Spain that the account of Vancouver's voyages had been published in London four years earlier, including his voyages to the northwest coast of North America. The Depósito Hidrográfico in Madrid was instructed to publish the narrative of Galiano's voyage, and did so just before the new war cancelled any plans that might have existed to publish accounts of other Spanish voyages.

A few years later Carlos abdicated and Napoleon Bonaparte installed his brother Joseph on the Spanish throne. When Bonaparte was overthrown the reactionaries in Spain regained control. By that time the wars of independence in Spanish America had started and when they were over the whole episode of the northern explorations from New Spain was forgotten. The main objective of the Spanish thrust to the north had been the discovery and control of the Northwest Passage. When the Passage was proved to be mythical by Galiano and Vancouver, the dust settled on the archives and the *Relación del Viage hecho por las Goletas Sutil y Mexicana en el Año de 1792 para reconcer el Estrecho de Fuca* became the only Spanish account known to the world.

Another account had slipped through the hands of the Spanish authorities although it had been officially suppressed before it had been circulated. In some way a copy of this account fell into the hands of an English writer. This was the journal of a voyage by Quadra in 1775. A translation appeared in a book of essays we will describe later. It seems to have attracted little public attention at the time, although the English explorers knew of it as early as 1778 and it is possible that this is the reason Captain Cook did not go through any ceremony to claim the land for Great Britain until he reached 61° North latitude.

The *Ilustración* lit only a small candle in Spain but its light did disclose these two documents which provide most of the contemporaneous published information on the first explorers and the first settlements between California and the Russian outposts in the far north.

2

THE NORTHWEST PASSAGE

M ichael Lok's story about the voyage of Juan de Fuca was neither the first nor the last account of a fictitious voyage, but it lasted longer than most. The Atlantic had been full of mythical islands which gradually disappeared from the maps as exploration was extended, but the Northwest Passage had a teleological resistance to the encroachment of geographical knowledge. Because of the barrier of Arctic ice and the perils of Cape Horn, the Northwest Passage would be enormously valuable to the nation which controlled it. A number of mariners claimed to have sailed through it (in various latitudes), some drew maps of their voyages, and when the English pirate Cavendish captured the galleon *Santa Ana* in 1587, the Spanish thought he must have sailed through the Passage and that the English were going to keep it to themselves. In fact he had captured a ship off Peru whose pilot told him the route and approximate schedule of the Manila galleons.[1]

The Russians had no great interest in a Northwest Passage, but they had been trading intermittently with the natives in Alaska since Bering's voyage in 1741. The Spanish were concerned that this might lead to a Russian establishment in Alaska and a push down the coast towards the Northwest Passage or even towards New Spain. Indeed, the Spanish ambassador in Moscow reported that the Russians planned to do this.[2]

This concern, as well as the need for a better sea route between Spain and its Pacific possessions centered on Manila, led the Spanish to think of exploring the coast north of Monterey where a mission had been established for some time. For nearly two centuries there had been unsuccessful attempts to push farther north.

The first Spanish expedition, and indeed the first European expedition to reach British Columbia, was that of Juan Perez, which left San Blas on January 24, 1774.[3] San Blas was the naval base on the Mexican west coast. Perez was in command of the frigate *Santiago*, built at San

Blas in 1772-3. Her normal complement was sixty-four men, but eighty-six were on board when she left, plus two priests and some artisans bound for Monterey. They got as far as San Diego when Perez decided to put into port. *Santiago* had a sprung hull plank; she needed new masts; she was becalmed; all these reasons are attributed to Perez by different writers of his time. In any event, he stayed in San Diego for twenty-five days before sailing for Monterey. Here he stayed for twenty-six days and was not ready to leave until June 6. Then the wind failed, and *Santiago* finally got under way on June 17.

These delays were to cost the expedition any chance it had of making a useful voyage. The orders were to proceed directly from Monterey to 60° North latitude, where a fictitious account by one Ferrer Maldonado in 1588 has placed the Strait of Anian, leading into the Northwest Passage. Perez discovered his water supply was running low when *Santiago* was at about 51° North. This is only one of a number of puzzling features of the voyage. They had left San Blas with a six months supply of water and presumably they could have topped up their supplies in Monterey which they had left only a month earlier. Perez decided to put in for water and he sighted land at the northern tip of what we know as the Queen Charlotte or Haida Islands, although his estimate of latitude was fifty miles off. The Indians came off in canoes to meet him, but Perez made no attempt to land in spite of his shortage of water. Instead he turned back south.

Still in search of water, he closed the land a week later and anchored at a place he called the Rada de San Lorenzo, which has been identified as being just north of Estevan Point, on Vancouver Island. This was later to be Cook's landfall, and the landfall of later Spanish explorers. Nearby was an Indian summer village at the place later called Friendly Cove by the English and Santa Cruz de Nutca by the Spanish. Some of the Indians came out in their canoes to meet them. This was the first contact between the native people of British Columbia and the Europeans, and the story was still current among their descendants in 1874 when Father Brabant established a mission at Hesquiat, not far away.

The Indians told Brabant that at first their ancestors had thought that *Santiago* was an immense bird, then that it was a canoe "come back from the land of the dead with their bygone chiefs."[4] One Indian tradition has it that the blocks used for tightening the rigging, which sailors call deadeyes, looked like skulls, so they thought the big moving island with trees was inhabited by dead men.[5] Neither immense birds nor dead chiefs seemed to deter them, because the barefoot Indians exchanged gifts with the strangely clad men with wooden feet.

Perez attempted to send the launch ashore to perform an act of possession and to obtain water, but had to abandon this when the wind got up and *Santiago* dragged her anchor. The ship was rapidly carried towards the shore, and they had great difficulty in getting the launch back aboard. They made sail, cut the anchor cable, and managed to get away to sea. Part of the difficulty was the lack of seamen who still had the strength to work. Many of the crew were down with scurvy.

Finally, they staggered into Monterey on August 27, with little water and two thirds of the crew incapacitated. Almost the only tangible accomplishment of this voyage was to transfer two silver spoons and some abalone shells to the Indians at the Rada de San Lorenzo. These articles were seen by Captain Cook four years later and formed part of Spain's case for its claim to the northern coast. The spoons were bought by one of Cook's officers and later given to Sir Joseph Banks in England.[6]

Interlude

UN ACTA DE POSESIÓN

I t took more than the evidence of a couple of silver spoons to lay claim to newly discovered lands. That required a formal act of possession, which Perez failed to do, an omission cited by the British to refute the spoon argument.

Many acts of possession were carried out later by Spanish officers, all of which followed a similar pattern. The first thing was to get ashore and carry out the prescribed ceremony. After the voyage of Perez all commanders did this. If there was a chaplain available a mass was said, on shore if it was considered safe, otherwise aboard ship. If there was no chaplain, the mass could not be said but a litany was sung.[1] Salutes were usually fired and any other ships in the vicinity were expected to reply. There would be cheers for the King of Spain and other patriotic outbursts. All these activities, however, were peripheral. The main thing was the Act of Possession itself. The example I have is from 1790 but there was not much difference between the various ceremonies.[2] This one was the Act of Possession performed by Manuel Quimper at the place he called the Rada de Valdés y Bazan, now known as Royal Roads, west of Victoria. Valdés y Bazan was the Navy Minister, and also Minister of the Indies (i.e., the American and Pacific Colonies) in Madrid.

I have a copy of the full text of this Act. It runs to 1048 words, not counting the signatures, so I will refrain from giving a full translation here.

It starts out by saying, "In the name of God ..." We are already up to 72 words, after going through the Trinity, Maker and Creator, and on to Glory and Honour.

"In the name of God," then, "be it known that on June 30, 1790 there arrived the sloop *Princesa Real* belonging to Carlos IV ...." We are now up to 209 words of which the last 96 are the name and titles of the king.

"... by orders of the Viceroy ..." 312 words gone by so far. As we move on from God to the king to the viceroy the names and titles get longer. "... the sloop left San Blas on the 3rd of February under command of Ship's Ensign Manuel Quimper and anchored at this roadstead, naming it Valdés y Bazan ..." 381 words thus far, only ten of which were needed for Quimper's name. "... having disembarked with most of the seamen and soldiers and carried ashore a Cross which they adored on their knees, the Commandant took possession, in the name of the King, of the land where they disembarked, noting that it already belonged to him by virtue of the free gift of the Pope in 1493, together with adjacent lands and waters ...." 711 words, without saying anything about where "adjacent" stops.

Next the scribe appointed by the Commandant, one Estevan Banales, describes their actions on shore. The Commandant took his sword in hand and cut trees, branches, and grass. He moved some stones about and walked on the ground and on the beach without anyone questioning or restraining him, or contradicting his right to do so. The troops were then formed up in martial order and carried the Cross in procession, singing a Litany. At the end of the procession they planted the Cross and made a mound of stones at its foot, in which a copy of the *Acta de Posesión* was placed, sealed in a bottle with pitch. The Cross was again adored and they stripped the bark off a tree, inscribing it with a cross and the initials of the Most Holy Name "INRI" and at the foot of the tree they inscribed *"Carolus IV Rex Hispaniarum."*

The reason for taking possession was also given. It was "to bring the Word of the Holy Gospel to the Barbarous Nations so that they might escape the snares of the Demon and their Souls might be saved."

On this occasion no barbarous souls in mortal peril were present, but at other places natives watched the proceedings without interfering and doubtless without having any idea of what was going on. Only the salute, if they hadn't heard one before, seems to have made an impression.

This rigmarole sounds futile to us, and in fact it was. When it came to the issue, a country could only maintain possession against other powers if it was prepared to go to war and if it won the war. Before dismissing the ceremony as nonsense, let us consider two points. First, although the Spanish ceremony was the most elaborate, all colonial powers went through some similar form of taking possession and set great store by it. Second, to be a Spaniard was to be a Catholic. The papal bull of 1493 which gave half the world to Spain was the word of God given through the Vicar of Christ, and the souls of the natives would burn eternally in Hell unless they received the benefits of the True Religion. These propositions would have been axiomatic to the Spaniards and there is no reason to suppose that they were other than deadly serious and absolutely convinced they were in the right when they carried the Cross in procession and slashed at trees.

THE FATAL LANDING

To pick up the story of the next Spanish voyage we have to go forward a few years and imagine ourselves in London. In 1781 anyone who called at the premises of B. White at Horace's Head, Fleet Street could have purchased a book by the Honourable Daines Barrington, Fellow of the Royal Society.[1] In those days the title of a book might take up half a page, but Barrington simply entitled it *Miscellanies*. The title was well chosen. It contained a number of papers on (among other subjects) the possibility of reaching the North Pole, the genealogy of the Kings and Princes of Wales from AD 688 to AD 1415, an account of Little Crotch who could play on the pianoforte "God Save Great George Our King" when nearly three and a half years old, an analysis of the reasons for the sudden decay of several trees in St. James's Park, an essay on the bat or reremouse, and a translation from the Spanish of the "Journal of a Voyage in 1775 to explore the coast of America north of California." The journal had been written by Francisco Antonio Maurelle, pilot of the King's Schooner *Sonora*. At the time of the voyage, Maurelle was just twenty years old.[2]

In 1781, Spain was at war with England but the journal, says Barrington, "having been placed in my hands for perufal I conceived it to be fo interefting for the improvement of Geography that I defired permiffion to tranflate it."

In January 1775, only a few months after Perez had returned to San Blas, Maurelle was in a ship in Vera Cruz, the principal port on the east coast of Mexico. He received orders from the Viceroy to proceed to San Blas to take up an appointment as pilot on an expedition then being prepared for exploration of the northern coast. After three hundred leagues of travel across Mexico he arrived in San Blas and met the commander of the expedition, Don Bruno Heceta (or Hezeta, or Eceta as the name is given in other accounts). Perez, who was not a commissioned officer, was relegated to the post of pilot of Heceta's ship this time.

The expedition consisted of a frigate and a schooner. Although Maurelle (or Mourelle) did not mention the name of the frigate, it was

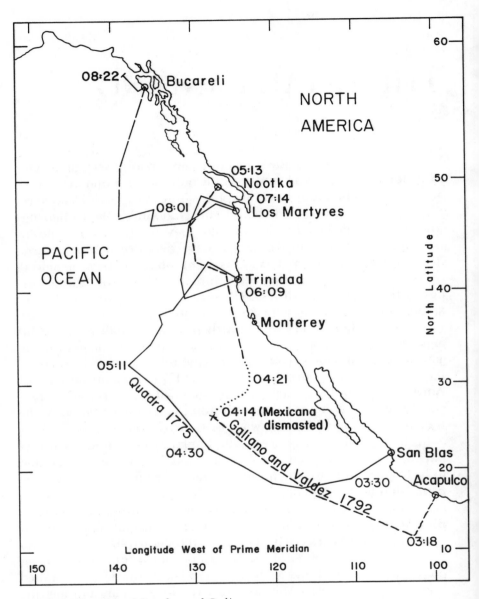

Northern Voyages of Quadra and Galiano.

the same *Santiago* which Perez had taken up the coast the previous year. This time there were ninety seamen in *Santiago*.[3] Maurelle was more interested in the schooner, because he was assigned to it. The *Sonora's* keel was only eighteen *codos* long (thirty-six Spanish feet) and the beam of the ship was six codos.

The commander was Frigate Lieutenant Juan de Ayala. His second in command was Frigate Lieutenant Juan Francisco de la Bodega, who was to become one of the important figures in the history of the Spanish period in British Columbia. Bodega's father had added his own mother's name to make the family name Bodega y Quadra. The English referred to him as "Quadra" and to save confusion we will do the same. Quadra was a *criollo,* that is a person of Spanish blood born in the Americas, in his case in Lima. He was probably thirty-one years old at the time.[4] The important posts in New Spain were held by *gachupines* as the criollos (or creoles) called the officials sent out from Spain and there was a mutual distrust and dislike between creole and gachupin. I do not know how much this distrust affected Quadra, but he volunteered for the junior position of second in command of the little *Sonora* with its crew of fourteen seamen of whom eight never returned to San Blas.[5] In addition there were three officers; Ayala, Quadra, and Maurelle, to whose journal we should now return.

They laid in a year's provisions and on March 16, 1775 they set sail. A supply ship destined for Monterey accompanied *Santiago* and *Sonora*. Only a few days out a signal of distress was made by the supply ship. A boat was sent over, which brought back the commander, who was obviously insane.[6] He was sent back to San Blas in a launch and Ayala was transferred to the supply ship and out of our story, leaving Quadra in command of *Sonora*. *Sonora* could not keep up with the frigate, which was forced to shorten sail to keep in touch. To make matters worse, *Sonora* sprung her foretopmast and had to heave to for repairs. Quadra tried various ways of improving the schooner's sailing qualities with only partial success. The frigate passed him a tow line and in this rather undignified way they limped along, working their way slowly to sea. With adverse winds and currents they were driven southward.

One day (March 31) they sailed or were driven by the current due south, already being well to the south of San Blas. It was over a month before they regained the latitude of their starting point, although by this time they were well out to sea. It is a pattern we shall see repeated in other voyages. They had by then reached the trade winds and were experiencing strong north easterlies which gave Quadra a chance to put *Sonora* to the test. He crowded on sail and the deck was constantly two planks under water which, said Maurelle "thoroughly convinced those on board the frigate of our determined resolution to prosecute our voyage." At least this is Barrington's translation of what Maurelle said. He took many liberties with the original, although Maurelle himself gave several accounts (all suppressed at the time) which varied in a number of details.[7] I have amended Barrington's account in places to conform to an abbreviated version in the Archivo General in Mexico.[8]

This determined resolution probably did not involve consultation with the crew, who were already beginning to fall sick. In the cramped miserable quarters on the schooner everyone was wet through except in calm weather, and Quadra could do little to help. He offered to transfer the sick to the frigate where there was a surgeon and medicines but the surgeon felt the risk of contracting fever during the transfer outweighed the advantages. Quadra gave the men small presents and reminded them of the glory they would obtain on their return. This is credited by Maurelle with producing a determination to live and die together.

By May 11 they were getting easterly winds with heavy squalls, but by then the south-flowing current had ceased to bother them and on the 21st they reached the latitude of Monterey, well out to sea. They were already two weeks behind the date at which Perez had reached Monterey the year before and the Viceroy had given orders they were to go to 65° North, having added five degrees to his instructions of the previous year. In spite of this Heceta wanted to go into Monterey, and called for a *junta* or council. One wonders whether Perez was advising him. The weather was too rough for Quadra to cross over to the frigate, so the junta was held by passing written opinions back and forth in a cask.

Barrington says that the opinions are given in the journal at length, but as they would not be interesting even to the navigator he did not translate them, only stating that it was agreed to proceed. Fortunately, Quadra recorded his opinion in his own journal.[9] He wrote that it was out of the question to go into Monte Rey and still give the best service to the King's interests. He proposed to go on to 42° latitude, to the inlet discovered by Martin de Aguilar. Here, wrote Quadra, the sick would recover as soon as they stepped ashore and there was no lack of water. In fact, all that was known of an inlet or river at this latitude was a report of its existence by the survivors of the Aguilar expedition in 1602, so Quadra was laying it on a bit thick. Quadra's mast and bowsprit were damaged, but he thought the lashings would hold. If not they could be replaced and, failing this, one could not expect to have every convenience on a voyage. If the purpose of putting in to Monte Rey was to make a new mast and bowsprit, this was tantamount to abandoning the voyage for the year, which would be a serious dereliction of service to his Majesty and would run counter to the instructions of His Excellency the Viceroy.

True, the schooner's timbers were split and incapable of holding a nail and she sailed so badly that Quadra had to crowd on more sail than was prudent, but this was the responsibility of those who had advised the Viceroy that the schooner was fit to sail and should not concern the captain or his pilot who, together with the crew, were determined to press on to 61° latitude in company with the frigate.

Faced with this somewhat unreasonable argument Heceta could do nothing but agree to go on. The voyagers crept northward, occasionally helped by a following wind but more often being forced to sail as close to the wind as they could. On June 1st they suffered their first casualty. One of the seamen thought glory was not enough and became so drunk with spirits that Quadra transferred him to the frigate where he died in spite of the surgeon's best efforts. Of his bones are coral made, like so many other nameless seamen. Maurelle gives more space in his journal to a description of some floating kelp which was found on the same day.

A few days later the tow-rope was abandoned after numerous breaks, but the difficulties in keeping station do not seem to have recurred. On June 7 they saw land, but were becalmed and carried south by the current. The frigate ordered *Sonora* to reconnoitre the coast and before nightfall Maurelle had seen many headlands, bays, beaches, mountains covered with trees, and green fields. It was water they wanted, and that they did not see, so Quadra stood out towards the frigate. Thus passed the night. The journal sticks to the facts, so the excitement at seeing this unknown land after two months at sea must be left to our imagination. The next morning they continued, and saw with the greatest clearness beaches, rocks, bays, headlands, breakers, and trees. Soon a high cape came in view, with a landlocked harbour south of it. Quadra asked the frigate to lend him a launch to sound the entrance. However, because of the freshening wind he could not get out to the frigate and Heceta was unwilling to send the launch because of the distance between the ships and the increasing seas.

The schooner crept in, sounding all the way, and the frigate followed in her wake. Quadra dropped an anchor "within a bow's shot of land" says Barrington. The version of Maurelle's journal which I have read calls it *un tiro de piedra*, a stone's throw. The ship was secured in the same way as a yachtsman might do it today. Finding some rocks ashore which nature seemed to have fixed there for the purpose, they

23

tied cables to them, then ran out another anchor at 45 degrees to the first. Only when the *contramaestre* or boatswain reported all secure did the skipper suddenly notice the silence which had descended after the creaking groaning splashing and cracking sounds which had been continuous for three months. Barrington did not translate the previous sentence because it wasn't in the original, but can things have changed much in two centuries?

Sonora had dropped her first anchor off a small village but the Indians did not send off any canoes until the ship was secured. Then they approached, wearing crowns of flowers and removing the strings from their bows.[10] After a while some of them came on board and offered skins in exchange for small articles. The Spaniards were too busy to pay much attention to the Indians at first and were also very much on their guard, but the unvarying kindness and friendliness of the Indians overcame the suspicion of the visitors. They were invited into all of the houses except that of the chief, although there seemed to be no difference between his house and the others. The roofs of the houses were at ground level. The doorway was a hole just large enough for one person, leading to a subterranean room. The floor was perfectly smooth and clean and the people warmed themselves around a fire built in a pit in the centre. There are remains of *kickwilli* houses in British Columbia which match this description, and you may visit a replica in the Provincial Museum in Victoria. There are similar house ruins in the eastern Arctic, remains of the Thule culture. The main difference between the Arctic houses and those described by Maurelle is that the Thules used whale bones and skins for the roof, instead of wood and earth.

Inside the house, it must have been a bizarre scene: the faces painted black and red, the firelight briefly showing the copper rings in the ears of the men. Now and then an arm covered with circular tattoos would make a gesture, or a woman with three great distensions of her lower lip would say something. The men had their legs and loins closely bound with strips of hide, but had no other clothing except furs which they wore in cold weather. The women were similarly dressed but added a fringed apron "about a foot wide."

The chief's rule was absolute (in Maurelle's opinion) but did not extend beyond his village. Each night the chief sent one of his men to the beach, presumably to make sure that all his own people were accounted for.

As word spread people came from other villages. The other Indians were not permitted to approach the local houses. The swarm of men, women and children amounted to several hundred people. One child, thought by Maurelle to be about a year old, had a bow and arrows of appropriate size and could hit a hand held up as a target from several yards away. The twenty-year-old Maurelle who had been at sea most of the time for five years may not have been a good judge of the ages of children.

An Indian died while Maurelle was there. After a funeral lament the body was burned, but Maurelle thought there was no religious significance to the lament. How could there be? The burning of the bodies of the dead showed that the Indians must have been "perfect atheists." Also, some of the men had several wives, and there were no idols or signs of sacrifices, which seemed to clinch the matter.

Their weapons were bows and arrows. Most of the arrows had flint heads, but some were of copper or iron. Iron was highly valued in trade, particularly knives or old barrel hoops. Maurelle was given to understand that the iron came from the north, but as far as he could make out the Indians had never seen white men before.

Maurelle was very conscious of the possibility of misunderstanding signs used as a substitute for language, and classed the above information as doubtful. The chaplain of the frigate reported one bit of sign language which did not seem to be ambiguous.[11] An Indian asked "with a significant gesture" whether the Spaniards were men like himself, which the Indians were unable to observe because Heceta had "prudently" ordered his men to have nothing to do with the women. That night two seamen were missing and had to be rounded up the next day. They paid for their "imprudent" night ashore with a flogging, which was curtailed because of protests by the Indians.

The main Indian foods were deer, otter, seal, and fish, and they ate everything but the bones and skin. If Quadra had only known he could have staved off the onset of scurvy by putting his men on the same diet. Vitamins are stored in the fat of animals and if you eat the whole beast or fish you don't need vegetables. This is not to say that the Indians were purely carnivorous: they also ate wild onions mixed with the leaves of a plant like parsley.

Maurelle laments his inability to learn more of Indian government, laws, and language, but I think he did pretty well, considering that they were only in the harbour they named Puerto de la Trinidad for eight days, and had to attend to all the work of taking on wood, water, and spars during that time. They also had to perform their act of possession to claim the land for Spain.

The two ships left Trinidad on June 19 and slowly worked their way westward to get clear of the northwest winds along the coast. Perez knew this tactic from his voyage in the previous year. Sonora's difficulties in keeping up with the frigate were reduced by some changes Quadra had made to her rig but, in spite of this, adverse winds forced them back in towards the coast after a few days, the alternative being to sail due south. Much fatigued by the violence of the weather, Maurelle again saw land on July 11, and also saw the frigate, which he had lost sight of several times. Adverse winds then forced the ships to turn south to keep off the rocks, so they stopped and anchored. Maurelle went across to the frigate. He said that all the crew on the frigate were sick. He was told to ask his commander to join a council to decide whether the risks of continuing the voyage were too great. Quadra decided to leave it until the next day. Maurelle's journal may have been written later and was probably edited after the voyage. One can detect signs of coming events here. The difficulties *Sonora* had in maintaining contact and Quadra's delay in joining the council set the scene for Maurelle's narrative of the ultimate separation of the two vessels.

Heceta was invited ashore to share an Indian feast but declined. He also declined some of the food which was brought out to his frigate, although he did send a party ashore to perform an act of possession.[12] Perhaps the seeds of the next day's tragedy were sown by these actions.

Quadra, on the contrary, exchanged civilities with the Indians and accepted a present of salmon, plus some meat from an animal he could not identify.

Water from several springs could be seen flowing over the sand at the other end of the bay. The dense forest offered the opportunity to cut some new spars, so it was decided to send a party ashore the next morning. Although the Indians around *Sonora* remained friendly Quadra sent a well armed party of seven men ashore led by Pedro Santa Ana, who was *Sonora's* contramaestre or boatswain. Just as Santa Ana's boat was being pulled ashore through the surf a crowd of several hundred Indians armed with spears and clubs leapt from the forest, ran across the beach, and overwhelmed the boat party. Two men flung themselves into the sea, there was one musket flash, then it was all over.

Interlude

EL CONTRAMAESTRE

Q*ue Dios te guarde, Pedro Santa Ana.* Your officers said you were the best and most reliable seaman in the crew. Did you die so far from your native land because of treachery, or did you or your shipmates unwittingly transgress against some powerful tabu? Were you less vigilant than you should have been because of the trust that had developed between you and the Indians at Trinidad? In those seconds on the beach before the club exploded that last blinding light in your brain, did you think of yourself, your family, or the men you had led into a trap?

I shall never know. In fact if you had returned safely home from your voyage no one would today know your name. The names of your officers, even the name of the schooner to which you did not return, are perpetuated in names given later to islands none of you ever saw. I cannot name an island for you, but I can go to the beach where you died and walk along the shore and think of you for a little while. And I can dedicate a book to you.

4

LA COSTA
SEPTENTRIONAL

After the battle on the beach, Quadra could do nothing except fire some futile rounds from his great guns, which did not reach the landing place. His only boat had been chopped up by the Indians on the beach. He could not even put to sea because the low tide showed that *Sonora* was surrounded by rocks and shoals. The tide was high at noon and he tried to sail out to the frigate, with only three men and a boy on deck. There were four sick men below but they could not help. The Indians came off in canoes and, to Maurelle's surprise, started to offer gifts and tried to entice them ashore; when this didn't work the Indians surrounded the schooner. Quadra and Maurelle picked up muskets and fired. The resulting deaths and damage to the canoes after several shots drove off the Indians. Finally *Sonora* anchored near the frigate. Maurelle was all for taking the frigate's launch with an armed party to exact vengeance, but his senior officers decided to play safe. There was no possibility, even in Maurelle's view, that any of the shore party was still alive and a revenge mission, although it might dissuade the Indians from attacks on future voyagers, would cost more Spanish lives.

Five men were transferred from the frigate to *Sonora* and the voyage was resumed.[1] A few days later Perez and his pilot's mate Revilla asked for another junta.[2] The junta (or council) was a procedure frequently used both during a voyage and in the vice-regal administration in Mexico. A junta could be requested by a junior officer as in this case, even to call in question the orders of his superior, but usually it was initiated by the senior officer to get the advice of his colleagues. In the examples we have, naturally, written opinions were submitted. Subordinates do not seem to have hesitated at putting forward views contrary to those of their superiors. At the conclusion of a junta the senior officer made the decision, although sometimes the way in which arguments were put forward forced a decision on him.

At the junta, wrote Quadra, Perez was of the opinion that the risks to Quadra's ship were too great and that they should all return to San Blas. This inspired Quadra to write another opinion which Barrington omitted as being uninteresting.

Quadra laid it on with a trowel this time.[3] He started by reminding Heceta that when they were in latitude 37°, Quadra had personally verified the carpenter's assertion that the timbers of his ship were rotten yet he still opposed the proposal to put into Monte Rey; and now here they were in latitude 49°. Although the schooner rolled too much and shipped water over the deck, this was to be expected in a small vessel. His improvements to the rig, along with constant watchfulness when sailing, had enabled the schooner to keep up with the frigate and arrive safely this far. Without the schooner, wrote Quadra, the frigate could scarcely go on alone and they were required to go to 65°. Hardships, casualties, accidents, and risks must be borne with resignation and determination when one is concerned about the service of H.M. and the credit of the Nation "which has entrusted us with an arduous enterprise. It would be unworthy of my courage," he wrote, "to give way on this occasion without grave reason. Made aboard the Schooner in 49° under sail. Juan Francisco de la Bodega y Quadra."

All Quadra says about the outcome of this junta is that "the navigation continued." Maurelle is equally vague. As the voyage to *La Costa Septentrional* (the northern coast) continued *Sonora* gradually lost touch with the frigate, and one suspects that the vagaries of wind and weather were helped by a few judicious changes of course. On August 5 Quadra decided to forget about the frigate and press on.

The decision, and the voyage to which it led, are almost incredible. The sea had got into their bread locker, much of their water supply had been lost due to storm damage, and now some of the crew were showing unquestionable signs of scurvy. Even if everyone had been healthy, *Sonora* would have been shorthanded and those that were able to work had to tend the sick as well as sail the ship. The season for sailing on the northern coast was getting short. Still they pressed north, and on August 16 they made their landfall at 57° North at a cape they called Cabo del Engaño. They landed and obtained some water, and fresh fish was provided by Indians without incident. *Sonora* could now muster only two men for each watch and the crew was suffering from the cold as well as scurvy and fever. The wind was right in their teeth and finally, in 58° North latitude, Quadra turned back.

With the wind behind them, they could follow the coast more closely and concluded that the strait described by Maldonado did not exist in these latitudes. This disposed of only one of the fictitious accounts of the Northwest Passage. *Sonora* entered a large bay and they anchored to rest for a while. The air was much warmer and there were no Indians to be seen although several huts were visible on the shoreline. Maurelle was sent ashore, well armed and one can be sure extremely vigilant. He collected as much water and firewood as *Sonora* could carry with no trouble. The bay was named Bucareli in honour of the Viceroy. It bears his name still. Here another act of possession was performed.

The voyage south was agony. There were more and stronger gales as September passed, which further damaged the ship. At one time there was only one seaman who could take the helm, while Quadra and Maurelle tended the sails. After two more men became convalescent the two officers both came down with fever, but had to show themselves on deck because of the despair of the crew. Now Quadra could not approach the coast too closely, because of the danger to the ship in the event of a wind change, with no one to handle the sails if they had to tack. They were within sight of the coast nearly all the way and peaks and headlands of Vancouver Island could be seen distinctly. Mapping was continued and *Sonora* reached Monterey on October 7 with everyone aboard suffering from scurvy.

Heceta's frigate *Santiago* was in Monterey. After losing touch with *Sonora* he had begun to get more petitions from Perez and other officers urging him to turn back. There was some reason for these petitions. About a third of the crew were down with scurvy so Heceta turned back to Monterey soon after he lost touch with Quadra.[4] During the voyage from Monterey to San Blas Perez died. Although his work seems timorous to us, he was the first European to reach the Pacific northwest coast and the first to meet the Haidas and the people of Vancouver Island.

It was not until 1779, a year after Captain James Cook had visited the place he called Nootka, that another Spanish voyage was undertaken, this time with the usual 5° of northing added to the instructions, making the objective 70° North. Two frigates were assigned. The expedition was led by Ignacio Arteaga, commanding the frigate *Princesa*, built in San Blas the previous year. *Princesa* ultimately made eight voyages to the northern coast, more than any other Spanish vessel.[5] Maurelle was assigned to *Princesa* as pilot.[6] The second frigate was *Favorita*, commanded by Quadra who had purchased it in Callao de Lima for the navy. This visit to his birthplace must have given Quadra great satisfaction as he had been promoted and decorated after the 1775 voyage. The pattern of the 1779 voyage was to become a familiar one: up to Alaska, look for Russians, look for the entry to the Northwest Passage, then back to San Blas with a few more acts of possession performed. The only difference this time was that on their return they found that Spain had openly entered the American War of Independence after giving clandestine support to the colonists for some time, and was at war with England. The war ended both Spanish and English exploration for the time, and left the Northwest Passage undiscovered.

The next Spanish voyage was not made until 1788. In that year two ships were sent north under the command of Esteban Josef Martinez. He had been a junior pilot with Perez as far back as 1774 but was not chosen for the 1775 voyage because of doubts as to his suitability. He had spent much of his time after that in sailing between Monterey and San Blas. The second ship was commanded by Gonzalo Lopez de Haro, who was making his first voyage to La Costa Septentrional. Quadra was serving in Europe at the time and did not return to New Spain until the next year.

Martinez is a strange figure. He was older than most of the mariners in the Department. He would have been forty-six to fifty-three years old in 1788 (reports as to his birth date vary) and he was still not a commissioned officer.[7] He quarrelled with his subordinates throughout the voyage and became violent on occasion. He seems to have been drunk a good part of the time when ashore. Nevertheless, he was the most experienced pilot in the Department, where he had been stationed for at least fifteen years, and was dedicated to the service and to the extension of Spanish settlement to the north. This was an idea on which Viceroys and Ministers had blown hot and cold.

In spite of frequent quarrels, the explorers reached the Alaskan coast, but Martinez became so abusive that Lopez de Haro headed westward on his own. He stopped at Kodiak Island where he met Evstrat Delarof, who was in charge of the Russian trading post that had been established there four years earlier.[8]

Martinez sailed right past Kodiak and reached Unalaska, the appointed western rendezvous. It is not clear to me how the Spaniards knew of this Russian outpost, but Spanish ministers in Moscow seemed to know what was going on in Russian territory, although little seemed to be known of British and American trading activities further south on the coast. When Lopez de Haro got to Unalaska he found Martinez living ashore with Potep Zaikov, whose fondness for Spanish brandy matched Martinez' enthusiasm for Russian vodka. At least, so said Lopez de Haro.[9] Martinez was too busy later on to give his version.

Lopez took the extreme step of withdrawing his ship from Martinez' command and heading back to San Blas to file a complaint with the

Viceroy.[10] Martinez stopped at Monterey on his way back, which was an appointed rendezvous, but eventually gave it up and headed for San Blas himself.

By the time Martinez returned, the Viceroy was much more interested in what he had to say about the Russians than in what he had to say about Lopez de Haro. The latter had already reported that the Russians were planning to occupy Nootka in 1789. Martinez confirmed this, having got the same story from Zaikov that Lopez got from Delarov.[11] Martinez may have said this because it supported his project for a settlement at Nootka, which no Spanish officer had seen since Perez anchored offshore in 1774 with Martinez as his pilot's mate.

All this lent support to a rumour that had been circulating for two years. In 1786 the French captain La Perouse had called in at a port in Chile on his way north. A French speaking Spaniard there found out that La Perouse was heading for Alaska and the Spaniard was shown a map which indicated Russian settlements at several points, including "Nootka."[12] The map was either based on surmise, or it was a distortion of an old Russian map. After La Perouse had been to Alaska (he never went near Nootka) Martinez, who happened to be at Monterey, escorted him into harbour and formed an impression that the Russians intended to occupy Nootka.[13]

Martinez may have invented some of this, but what he said reinforced a legend. An invention in support of a legend has the power of truth without its limitations. Apprehension of rival claims from the English may also have influenced the Viceroy. Early in 1789 he decided to move, possibly without even waiting for word from Madrid.[14] He gave orders to establish a fortified settlement at Nootka under the command of Martinez.

Interlude

CHIRIKOV'S MEN

The legend reinforced by Martinez was that a Russian settlement in the latitude of the Strait of Juan de Fuca had been in existence for over forty years at the time Martinez was preparing to leave for Nootka. Had this legend been true, it would have been the first European settlement on the west coast of what is now Canada.

As with many legends, it started as a true story. In 1741 two captains in the Russian service sailed from Kamchatka, a small village on the Siberian coast.[1] They were Vitus Bering and Alexei Chirikov. The two captains separated to explore the Alaskan coast and the Aleutian Islands, which Bering had seen in 1728. This time, Bering explored the strait now bearing his name and there he lost his life. Chirikov headed further south, ran down his eastings to the coast, then turned northwards. On his way he stopped at an island which was probably at the north end of the Alexander Archipelago. He sent ashore a party of ten seamen, plus his pilot Avraam Demente'ev. They carried arms, and also had a small cannon and two signal rockets. Six days passed with no sign of boat or men. Chirikov suspected boat trouble so sent a carpenter and a caulker ashore in the only other boat he had. The boatswain, Sidor Savel'ev and a seaman named Fedeev volunteered to go with them to see what lay ashore.

That was the last Chirikov saw of his fifteen crew members. Some of the natives came off in their boats, making ambiguous gestures, but could not be induced to come on board. Finally, Chirikov did the only thing he could. He sailed back to Kamchatka.

It was inevitable that speculation on the fate of the men would harden into a legend that they had survived. There was talk of a rescue mission, but Russia had almost no ships in the Pacific and no nation could go looking for all its poor lost seamen in those days. James Cook was off the coast in 1778 but stayed offshore. Russian maps in 1781 showed a bay at 53°20' North labelled as Demente'ev's landing place, but this was probably just an attempt to discourage the Spaniards. In 1774 Perez reported seeing Indians with white skins at about this same latitude. He said they had some copper implements and iron weapons

33

which had been made from an old bayonet and part of a sword, although all his chaplain saw was an object he "thought was an iron axe."[2] These items, assuming they were as reported, could have been transferred southward by intertribal trade and might have come originally from the Chirikov expedition, if not from the lost men.

Perez was not the only one to notice fair-skinned Indians. One of Cook's officers said that some were "as fair as any Europeans with a good colour in their cheeks" when washed clean, although another thought that the brightness was due to contrast with the dark colour of the oil and dust which covered their bodies.[3] When one of the women was washed clean from head to foot she looked much darker than when only a small patch of clean skin was visible.[4]

The next development in the story of Chirikov's men was a neat bit of circular legendry. The Russian ambassador in Madrid sent to Moscow a lengthy account of the 1788 voyage by Martinez and Lopez de Haro. The original has been lost, but someone in the Moscow bureaucracy made what we would call an "executive summary" of it. The summary said that Martinez encountered "eight Russian settlements along the coast between 48° and 49° latitude." This is probably a deliberate or careless change from the original. Chirikov himself had given the latitude of the place where the men were lost as 57° 30′ and the Russians knew perfectly well where their own settlements were. The Chief Manager of the Russian trading venture seized on the opportunity to advertise these settlements between 48° and 49°, occupied by Chirikov's descendants. He wanted no Spaniards north of California.

As late as 1819 the Russians were still giving instructions to their navigators to search the Strait of Juan de Fuca for the Russian settlements. The instructions were never carried out but the Russian government used the legend to support their arguments on the southern limit of Russian territory.

No one knows what happened to Chirikov's men but it is pretty clear that none of them reached British Columbia, that Perez and Quadra were the first Europeans to do so, and that Martinez was the first to set up an establishment on shore.

5

MARTINEZ IN COMMAND

It was almost accidental that the little bay called Friendly Cove was chosen as the site of the first place between Alaska and California where Europeans would live. Perez anchored nearby in 1774 for no better reason than that he sighted land and needed water. Four years later Cook was feeling his way up the coast and the fog happened to lift when he was at the same place. Later Cook's officers discovered the value of sea otter pelts in Canton, so when traders, including some of Cook's officers, went in search of pelts they naturally started at the same place. They also knew the Indians there, and had enjoyed good relations with them, and in particular with Maquinna who was their chief. Although the Spanish do not seem to have known much about the English merchantmen, they knew of Cook's visit through the published account of his last voyage. So Martinez was dispatched to Nootka.

He was given the frigate *Princesa* and the supply ship *San Carlos*, the latter commanded by Lopez de Haro, in spite of the row they had had the year before. He was also given a set of instructions which reflect a certain nervousness about the commission.[1] He was to go to Nootka and take possession for Spain. He was to build a great hut ashore for shelter, protection and trading and, if anyone came along, he was to claim he was establishing a formal settlement. The purpose of the hut was to establish Spain's rights. Martinez was to retire to his ships at night and stay at Nootka until he received further orders.

He was exhorted not to fall into harsh language and to treat any English or Russians with tact and civility, although he was to explain to them the equity of Spain's claim to sovereignty. He could be a lot firmer with any Americans who might happen along, using "stronger arguments." He was only to use force against foreigners if they used it first, and even then he should do this without encroaching on their rights.

All this is like telling the fox to go and play quietly in the chicken run. We do not know why such impossible instructions were given to a man as erratic and violent as Martinez. The only reason he was chosen for the commission was that the Viceroy wanted to buy time until he heard from Madrid and he had no one better than Martinez for the job. The Viceroy at this time was Flores, a man who is not remembered for his brilliance or determination. Martinez claimed that Flores was his uncle, but he was given to making such claims to impress people, since his rank of Alferez (a noncommissioned officer junior to a lieutenant) was not an exalted one.

Whatever the reasons for Martinez' appointment, the results were disastrous. There are many accounts of the events at Nootka that summer, but I will tell it as Martinez did in his own journal.[2] He arrived at Friendly Cove on May 5, 1789, where he found a ship at anchor. Martinez hoisted his Spanish flag and fired a salute. This was the first cannon shot at Nootka that season and a great deal of gunpowder was consumed before the season ended. On one day one hundred and sixty shots boomed out over the hitherto quiet bay. From first to last not one shot was fired in anger. They were all salutes.

The anchored ship returned the salute and hoisted Portuguese colours. It turned out to be the *Ifigenia*. The nominal captain was a Portuguese named Viana, but the ship carried an English supercargo, William Douglas, and all the crew were English.

We have to go back a bit to find out how the *Ifigenia* came to be at Nootka in 1789. Martinez, naturally, didn't know this part of the story. It started with a certain John Meares.[3] Meares was a half-pay (i.e. unemployed) lieutenant of the navy of His Britannic Majesty who was operating as a merchant captain. He was fronting for a group of officers of the East India Company in Calcutta. No one was allowed to trade in the Pacific without a licence from that company, which held a monopoly granted by King George. The monopoly could not be enforced against foreigners, but as far as possible it was enforced against English ships. The group in Calcutta devised a scheme to cheat their own employer. Meares was engaged as a partner and a ship was acquired, nominally under his ownership. He set off for the American coast in 1786, but it was late in the season and he was forced to winter in Prince William Sound. In addition to the normal miseries of a winter on the Alaska coast the crew began to come down with scurvy and twenty-three of them died during the winter.

In the spring of 1787 Meares encountered the *King George* under the command of Nathaniel Portlock, who had been one of Cook's officers and was now engaged in the fur trade. Portlock had a proper licence from the East India Company, but instead of seizing Meares' ship as he was entitled to do, he took pity on the utter misery of his crew and gave

Meares supplies to complete his voyage. While this meeting was most fortunate for Meares and his surviving crew, it posed a problem for his backers in Calcutta.

It was realized that they could not continue their venture under the British flag so another scheme was concocted. In 1788, Meares was given two ships. He then left for Macao, a Portuguese colony, and in exchange for one share in the venture a Portuguese named Juan Cavalho became the nominal owner of the ships. This not only avoided the cost and restrictions of a licence from the East India Company but also enabled the ships to take advantage of a preferential tariff in Canton negotiated by the Portuguese. One of these ships was the *Ifigenia*.

During the 1788 trading season, Meares encountered other ships properly licenced by the East India Company, who were not taken in by the disguise. At the end of the season he set off for Canton, but he sent the *Ifigenia* to Hawaii for the winter, with orders to meet him again at Nootka in the spring of 1789.

Not only was Martinez ignorant of all this, but William Douglas, nominally the supercargo but in fact the captain of the *Ifigenia*, didn't know that while he had been in Hawaii Meares and his group had realized their rascally scheme had run its course and had gone legitimate by licencing their ships and merging their interests with the other licencees. Hence the Portuguese colours which Douglas hoisted in reply to Martinez' salute.

There was an interested spectator on hand. This was Captain John Kendrick of the Boston ship *Columbia*. He and his fellow American captain Robert Gray of the *Lady Washington* had wintered nearby and their ships were then anchored in a bay seven miles away which was a more convenient place for making repairs.[4]

Let us return to Martinez' account. He asked Douglas for his papers. Douglas produced a Portuguese passport which included instructions to Viana (the nominal Portuguese captain) to resist any attempt at seizure and to "take possession of any ship which molests you, and of its cargo, bringing its officers to Macao for punishment as pirates."[5]

Martinez ruminated for a day or two, then seized the *Ifigenia*. He did not interfere with Kendrick. He should have ruminated a bit longer, because he had no men to spare to take the *Ifigenia* to San Blas. Finally he released ship and crew, taking a bond drawn on the owners for the value of the ship if she should be declared a lawful prize, and told Douglas to head back to Macao. Douglas was only too pleased to comply.

Another ship showed up soon after. This was the *Princess Royal,* commanded by Thomas Hudson. She was another of Meares' ships. According to Martinez, Hudson said he had come for wood and water, and to effect some repairs to his ship, so Martinez gave Hudson some assistance and then told him he was free to leave for Macao. Kendrick and his partner Gray were still around and later moved their ships to Friendly Cove, but with them Martinez did not use any of the "strong arguments" referred to in his instructions. The Brits have suggested that Kendrick secured Martinez' friendship with a strong argument of his own, a good supply of rum which Martinez was welcome to share.[6]

Martinez was busy during this time at his appointed task of building structures to secure Spain's rights. He built a fort on the island at the entrance to Friendly Cove and mounted guns in it. He took a moment to record in his journals the death of José Jacinto de la Mota who was the *sangrador* or blood-letter. Medical services then became the responsibility of Juan Gallardo, who was appointed to fill the vacancy. It was as well to remain healthy on those voyages. Work on the "great hut" was under way when Martinez remembered something. He performed an act of possession to claim sovereignty for Spain. *Mas vale tarde que nunca,* or as we would say, better late than never.

As if poor Martinez hadn't had enough of foreign ships yet another one showed up. It was the *Argonaut,* another of Meares' fleet, commanded by a Captain Colnett who had been a midshipman on Cook's second voyage to the South Pacific. Colnett told Martinez (according to the diary of the latter) that he was empowered by the King of England to take possession, to establish a fortified trading post at Nootka, and to prevent anyone else from engaging in the fur trade. The *Argonaut* showed no colours and because of his ambiguous standing it seems that Colnett had no wish to raise any, so Martinez raised the Spanish flag and fired a salute. He waited a while. Nothing happened aboard the *Argonaut,* so Martinez sent a boat over to say it would be considered an insult if *Argonaut* did not reply. A reluctant blank charge was inserted in an unwilling gun and an unruly halliard finally consented to raise at the mainmast a blue pennant with a white square which looked to Martinez somewhat like an English commodore's pennant. This pennant was supplemented by "blue English flags" at bow and stern.

The trouble with this part of the story is that no reliable person recorded what happened. I repeat what Martinez put in his diary which differs noticeably from the version later given to the British government by Meares, who is no more to be believed than Martinez. According to Martinez, he asked Colnett for his papers, which Colnett said had been mislaid. Finally Colnett showed Martinez a document which he said was a Portuguese passport but refused to hand over either the passport or his instructions, which he said were in a confidential document he had received from his King (of England, not Portugal).

Martinez said in his report that Colnett put his hand on his sword and he said something which sounded to Martinez like "God damned Spaniard." So Martinez arrested him and seized his ship. At this point Martinez may have regretted all the lobbying he had done to promote a settlement at Nootka under his command.

We may picture the scene at Nootka. Colnett was under guard, his men were prisoners, his ship was seized and searched which revealed the instructions — not from King George but from Meares — and the two Americans, Kendrick and Gray, were watching the play unfold. It was the fourth of July, and after the usual salutes in honour of the United States Kendrick invited all the officers over for a drink to celebrate the fourteenth birthday of his country. What about Colnett? He came too. After all, he was an officer.

Martinez had sent one of his pilots, Narvaez, off to the south soon after his arrival at Nootka. Narvaez now returned to report that he had discovered the Strait of Juan de Fuca. It had been more than adequately discovered by this time. Although it had not been discovered by de Fuca it had been discovered by Barkley (as we have seen) and by Meares (in conversation with Barkley). Charles Duncan drew a view of the entrance in 1788 when he was in command of *Princess Royal* although Martinez probably did not know this.[7] Martinez himself said he had seen it in 1774, from a distance. Narvaez's report gave Martinez back some of his confidence. He thought there were grounds for believing that "the Strait connected both with the Mississippi and with the Strait of Fonte whose two mouths lie in latitudes 54° 23' North and 52°." Not "may lie" or "might lie." They "lie" in those latitudes.

Hudson turned up again in the *Princess Royal*. He had not gone to Macao, but had gone trading and was now back looking for Colnett. Martinez had now passed the point of no return, so into the *calabozo* went Hudson.

Martinez could not bring himself to use the tact and respect mentioned in his instructions, but at least he was acting in what he thought was the best interest of his country. There had been no violence in spite of the angry exchanges with Colnett. On July 13 an incident occurred for which I can find no excuse. A chief named Kelekem, who was a relative of the Nootkan chief Maquinna, came alongside and for some reason made some insulting remarks to Martinez. Martinez, according to his own diary, picked up a musket and pulled the trigger, but it misfired. One of his sailors seeing this, took another musket and shot Kelekem dead. Martinez later claimed that he had intended to fire over Kelekem's head. His diary says that he fired at Kelekem. It also says that the affair was Colnett's fault, because he had told Kelekem he was going to drive Martinez out of Nootka. Martinez' reasoning is hard to follow here.

By this time, there was no point in continuing the pretence of establishing a settlement as ordered by the Viceroy. The men were put to work building accommodation for the prisoners aboard the *Argonaut*. This was well under way on July 15 when Kendrick and Gray left "to continue their voyage of discovery."

Two weeks later a Spanish ship, the *Aranzazu*, arrived with orders. Martinez was to pack up and return to San Blas before the winter. This order had been written only a week after Martinez sailed for Nootka and Flores may later have forgotten about it.[8] When Martinez got back to San Blas he was asked why he had left Nootka. *Aranzazu* left on August 15, following the seized ships to San Blas, but Martinez lingered until the end of October. He had written a plea to the Viceroy to let him stay on and was hoping for a favourable reply.[9] Whatever faults Martinez may have had he certainly was not afraid of bad weather and he was dedicated to the establishment of a settlement at Nootka. The Viceroy's orders had to be obeyed, of course, so Martinez finally sailed back to San Blas.

Flores had a real mess on his vice-regal hands. He had a batch of British subjects arriving at San Blas as prisoners, along with some of the Chinese (or possibly Sinhalese) artisans whom Colnett had brought to Nootka to build his trading post. He had three English ships which didn't belong to him — the two seized ships as well as the *Northwest America* built by Meares at Nootka in 1788. It had been forcibly seized (Meares) or else repaired and made seaworthy after having been found rotting and abandoned (Martinez). When the Brits heard about it undoubtedly all hell would break loose in London. Soon he also had an American ship. Just before leaving Nootka, Martinez had seized a schooner named *Fair American*.

Flores rose to the occasion. He put the prisoners on the Spanish payroll and had the ships repaired.[10] He referred the question of lawful prize to Madrid and he had Martinez' report placed in the correct file, fortunately for History. He then settled down to wait for his successor to arrive and take over.

Interlude

THE NOOTKA DISPUTE

When Meares heard about the commotion at Nootka, he devised a shrewd counter-measure. He addressed a memorial to the House of Commons. Since this has been described elsewhere and I am telling the Spanish story I won't go over it in detail.[1] The memorial made no mention of the Portuguese flag or of the nominal Portuguese captain, Viana, but it did say that Meares was working in conjunction with "several British merchants residing in India" and that he purchased land from Maquinna whereon he erected a house and hoisted British colours in 1788. He claimed that he had purchased an exclusive trading licence from Wickaninish, who was Maquinna's brother-in-law, and that Colnett was sent "to erect a substantial house on the spot ... purchased the previous year." He then described the seizure of the ships and said all articles of value were stolen from them. He did not mention the seizure of any buildings but said Martinez performed an act of possession at the site of Meares' "temporary house" on the lands purchased from Maquinna.

Righteous indignation at Martinez' insult to the British flag was described at the time in sufficient detail for me to omit it. Nor will I go into the grief of George III when the affair was reported to him, or the expressions of loyalty to His Majesty who was in fact declining into insanity. Since Carlos IV in Madrid was not a great king in the mould of his father, the real contest was between the Spanish Prime Minister Floridablanca and the younger Pitt, who was the Prime Minister in London.

Ten days after Martinez seized Colnett and his ship, an event occurred in Paris which was the real key to the Nootka affair. The Bastille was overrun by revolutionaries. By the time Meares presented his memorial to the House of Commons, Louis XVI had been forced to concede a constitution and was under the control of the newly-born National Assembly. It was an ideal time to break up the "Family Compact" between the Bourbons. Carlos IV was a descendant of Louis XIV, as were his queen Maria Luisa and Louis XVI (who were first cousins).

Pitt demanded satisfaction or war. Floridablanca asked Carlos IV to call on cousin Louis for help, but the National Assembly would not permit this and Louis had to answer that it was impossible. So Spain had to face England alone, with serious if unfounded worries about the possibility of a revolution in Spain similar to that in France.[2] The Spanish empire sprawled over the whole coast of the Gulf of Mexico, most of South America, and the North American west coast. In addition there were the islands in the Pacific and the Caribbean. It was too much to defend so Floridablanca gave in. The result was the Nootka Convention, virtually dictated by Fitzherbert, the British Ambassador in Madrid.

It is uncertain whether there would have been a war if Floridablanca had refused to give in. Preparations were certainly made in England and a lot of Englishmen including George III were persuaded that war was inevitable if Spain resisted. However, at about the same time Pitt tried a similar ramp against Russia over a Black Sea port and gave it up when Catherine the Great snarled back.[3]

The problem for Fitzherbert was not that Madrid might have resisted him. It was that no one in Europe, not even Meares, knew much about what had happened at Nootka in 1789. Accordingly the Nootka Convention required that the "buildings and land ... of which British subjects were dispossessed about the month of April 1789" be restored to their owners. The "buildings" or rather building, and also the British subjects, were long gone when Martinez arrived at Nootka in May rather than April 1789. The roof of the building had been used for firewood on the American ships which wintered nearby[4] and the extent of land purchased by Meares was not specified in his memorial.

Just reparation was to be made for acts of violence or hostility. Seized property, including ships, was to be restored to its owners or if it could not be restored, just compensation was to be paid. There was no provision as to how "just" compensation was to be determined but in ignorance of what had happened this was probably the best Fitzherbert could do.

It was agreed, by the much quoted Article V of the Convention, that to the north of the parts of the coast already occupied by Spain both parties should have free access. This clause turned out to be impossible to interpret when the commissioners for the two parties met later at Nootka.

Among the doubtful points was the matter of "both parties (having) free access." Did this mean "to the exclusion of all other nations?" The Spanish Viceroy thought it did.[5] If so, what would a hypothetical English or Spanish commander do when one of the numerous American traders came into port? Fortunately the question is hypothetical, because Spain withdrew and the English did not establish themselves on the northwest coast for another fifty years. By that time it was the colony of Vancouver Island.

6

THE *ESTABLECIMIENTO* AT NOOTKA

While Martinez was at Nootka "claiming" to build an establishment there, the second Count of Revilla Gigedo was sent to New Spain to replace Flores as Viceroy. He arrived at Vera Cruz in August 1789 but stayed there for several months and did not take over from Flores until they met in October.[1] Although the Nootka Convention lay in the future Revilla Gigedo released the *Fair American* on the grounds that it had not encroached on Spanish possessions. The released vessel sailed to Hawaii. Captain and all but one of the crew were killed by the natives of those paradisial islands soon after they arrived so there was no American left to write a memorial or claim compensation. It was not until July 1790, when word of the impending Nootka Convention reached Mexico, that the rest of the ships and prisoners were released.[2] Without waiting for this, Revilla Gigedo had decided soon after his arrival, that there should be no more "pretence" and that an *establecimiento* or fortified outpost should be set up at Nootka. Ironically, a royal order to this effect which said Nootka should be occupied and defended against all comers had been issued before Martinez had reached Nootka the previous year, but it did not arrive in Mexico. Martinez was condemned for actions conforming to instructions he never saw.

Francisco de Eliza was placed in command of the new expedition. He was given the frigate *Concepción* and the supply ship *San Carlos* along with *Princesa Real* which was the sloop *Princess Royal*, seized by Martinez.[3] Eliza got a good start on the season by leaving on February 3. Two more frigates, *Princesa* and *Aranzazu*, followed later. This was the most formidable Spanish force to travel to the northern coast thus far. There was also a company of soldiers aboard, seventy-five members of the Catalonian Volunteers under Pedro Alberni. Captain "Pere" Alberni was a Catalan himself. He had been with the company in New Spain for seventeen years.[4] *Princesa* was commanded by Jacinto Caamaño and his journal is the source of my account of life in the establecimiento during the first year.[5] On his arrival in April Eliza found, to his relief, that Nootka was deserted. By the end of June, when Caamaño arrived in *Princesa*, construction ashore was well under way.

There was good weather in July and storehouses were built so the ships could be unloaded. August was wet and Juan Soler, boatswain of *Concepción*, died, followed soon by Jines Saldran, a seaman. They were buried ashore. In September the buildings were pretty well complete, including a bakery (apparently there wasn't too much left of the buildings erected by Martinez) and workshops. The battery built by Martinez on the island at the entrance of the harbour was restored and fitted with guns.

A small schooner had been brought in the ships in pieces, and a crew had been working on it during the summer. It was launched during September and later christened *Saturnina*. This is thought by some to be a rebuilt version of Meares' schooner *Northwest America*, but the references in Caamaño's journal and in Eliza's instructions indicate it was brought to Nootka in pre-cut pieces and assembled there.[6]

During the summer, two expeditions were sent out. One was to probe the inlets to the south, particularly the Strait of Juan de Fuca. This was led by Manuel Quimper, using the *Princesa Real*. Quimper first explored the inlets on Vancouver Island. He didn't know it was an island and was looking for possible entries to the Northwest Passage. He then turned his attention to the Strait of Juan de Fuca, exploring it as far as the screen of islands at its eastern end.

Quimper mapped the strait, performing acts of possession at the ports of Revilla Gigedo (Sooke Harbour), the Rada de Valdés (Royal Roads), Córdoba (Esquimalt), Quadra (Port Discovery) and, on his way back, Nuñez Gaona on the southern shore. His ceremony at the Rada de Valdés is my model for an "Acta de Posesión" described earlier. If such acts had carried any weight this should have been enough to determine Spain's sovereignty over the Strait and its bordering lands. Quimper saw and named, but did not explore, the Ensenada de Caamaño. This is the present Admiralty Inlet, which leads into Puget Sound, but he thought it was just an Ensenada or bay.

The second expedition under Salvador Fidalgo was sent north. This voyage more or less repeated Martinez' 1788 trip, although he, Fidalgo, spent less time drinking with the Russians he met at a number of places. He had his "Acts of Possession" manual along and did his best to establish Spanish sovereignty on the Alaskan coast.[7] He could find no entrance to a Northwest Passage, and couldn't or didn't put in to Nootka on his way back.

The hospital at Nootka was completed during October and the sick were transferred ashore. On the 29th the first snow fell, and the realities of winter on the northern coast began to make themselves felt. The Indians all left for their winter quarters at the head of the inlet they and we call Tahsis.

In November a soldier of Alberni's company named Agustine Vicente died, and the next month another soldier, Josef Ramos, and a seaman named Juan Perdomo followed him to the graveyard at Nootka.

They had a visitor in January. It was none other than Colnett in the *Argonaut*. He had come to repossess the *Princess Royal* but like Fidalgo, Quimper had not called at Nootka after his expedition, returning directly to Monterey. Instead of seizing Colnett's ship, this time the Spaniards helped him to careen and repair it and later saw him off on his way to the "San Duic" Islands.

January 1791 was a month of constant snow and February one of constant rain. The supply of ship's biscuits ran out and the people had to be given fresh bread: surely no hardship.

In March the number of men in hospital increased to thirty-two and Eliza decided this was putting too much strain on the facilities at Nootka. In consequence a shelter was built on the upper deck of *Princesa* for the sick men, and, as well, a cabin for the sick Lieutenant Jaulia of the Catalonian Volunteers. Caamaño was ordered to take them back to Monterey. Not long after they left Nootka, Jaulia died.[8] There were a number of diseases. Scurvy was treated with some success by giving the victims an infusion of the shoots of the fir tree as well as other medicine. A variety of ailments described as "fever" was treated with an assortment of remedies. The deaths were mostly due to "bloody dysentery," perhaps cholera: it was invariably fatal.

Caamaño added notes on the Indians to his journal, but we will consider these later, along with notes by other observers.

As Caamaño was working his way south, he crossed a supply ship heading for Nootka. In addition to bringing the next year's supplies it brought Eliza his orders for the year. They were labelled "Ynstrucci-ónes Secretas" dated February 5, 1791, and they came from the Viceroy.[9] The instructions are clear enough for me to suspect that Quadra, who had returned to his native continent and was now the commandant at San Blas, had a hand in drafting them, but they contain one serious flaw. They are far too ambitious.

Eliza was instructed to make an exact map of the whole coastline from Bucareli Bay (now in Alaska) to Puerto de la Trinidad (north of San Francisco). He was to pay particular attention to the Strait of Fonte (which did not exist), the entry of Heceta (which did exist; it was the mouth of the Columbia River), various inlets near Nootka and the innermost parts of Fuca Strait. He was to do this himself, leaving Caamaño in charge at Nootka. Caamaño's departure for Monterey with the sick could of course not have been anticipated in Mexico, but it did leave Eliza with only one frigate. The supply ship was to return to San Blas with any sick men, maps of the explorations of the previous year, and any sea otter skins obtained in trade. Eliza was reminded that these were the property of the King. If Eliza could spare one of the frigates, Quadra would like to have it back.

If Eliza came across any English he was to be nice to them. The Viceroy thought that a peace was signed with England, and enclosed some sealed instructions, to be opened only if Eliza got the word that the peace had been signed.

There were the usual housekeeping instructions, including a reminder that any comforts issued to the men from stores should be charged against their pay.

Finally there was a post script dated March 12. Peace *had* been signed and Eliza was to open his sealed instructions. It appears that these did not have much bearing on the explorations that had been ordered, because Eliza set out to do what he could and explain why he couldn't do more.[10] He disposed quickly of the instructions concerning Alaska. Leaving Ramón Saavedra in charge at Nootka he put to sea in the supply ship *San Carlos*, in company with the schooner assembled during the previous year, the *Saturnina*. Immediately he discovered that winds were adverse, time was short and Alaska was out of the question, so he turned south. He sent the schooner into Nitinat (Barkley Sound) to make sure that it didn't lead inland and headed his own ship for the Strait of Juan de Fuca.

From Córdoba, which was the farthest point east reached by Quimper the previous year, Eliza sent a launch away to explore the channels through the islands Quimper had seen, but the launch crew were chased out by a large number of Indians. At this time the schooner *Saturnina* rejoined Eliza, having completed the examination of Nitinat. She was commanded by José Mariá Narvaez, who in the end did most of the exploring that year, since his small ship was much easier to handle in the tortuous channels among the islands. The launch, under the pilot Pantoja, did some useful work within its limited radius of action.

Eliza shifted his base across the Strait to the Puerto de Quadra. He found that Quimper's Ensenada de Caamaño was an inlet and renamed it Boca de Caamaño but he didn't explore it, thus missing Puget Sound. Narvaez worked his way through the Boca de Fidalgo and emerged into the Gran Canal de Nuestra Señora del Rosario. We call it the Gulf of Georgia, but a bit of the old name has been transferred to the Boca de Fidalgo, which is now Rosario Strait.

It is almost certain that Narvaez was the first European to enter the Gulf of Georgia, although some people believed an unlikely story by Meares to the effect that Gray had not only done this but had returned to the sea north of Nootka.[11] Gray himself denied this. Narvaez could see two islands to the north at the entrance of a *boca* five leagues wide. He could not approach them because of adverse winds and a strong current which set him away from the land. He found fresh water two miles out to sea and inferred there must be a large river emptying out through the boca. He named the islands "Cepeda" and "Lángara" and the inlet he called the "Canal de Floridablanca" after the man who had been prime minister of Spain the last time he had political news. Narvaez stayed with the eastern shore and got as far as Cape Lazo near the northern end of the Gulf. His supplies were getting low, so he turned back to rejoin Eliza, following the western shore most of the way. Since a year's stores for two frigates and the shore establishment had been brought to Nootka in the ship Eliza was using, it is strange that the expedition should have run short. Eliza says he had scurvy aboard, but it is not at all clear why this should have happened.[12] For whatever reason, the shortage of supplies forced them to return to Nootka where the gardens planted and tended by Alberni's Catalonian Volunteers were ready to harvest.[13]

At the same time, another voyage to Alaska was taking place. This consisted of the corvettes *Descubierta* and *Atrevida*, commanded by Alejandro Malaspina. Although Malaspina called at Nootka and Acapulco on his way back, he was not part of the Viceroy's team. He was on a voyage which was intended to go around the world making scientific studies, a voyage which had left Spain in 1789.[14] He had turned up at Acapulco early in 1791 and diverged from his planned route to do the standard Alaska Tour: look for Russians, the entry into the Northwest Passage, and gold or precious stones. Time after time, Spanish explorers were sent to do the same thing, suffering the same diseases and similar deaths. One should never underestimate the strength of a fixed idea in a bureaucracy.

There is little information on the next winter at Nootka. Eliza's reports say that although the weather was more severe than the winter before, there was much less disease. All of the vegetables which the Catalonian Volunteers had planted grew as well as they did in Andalusia except for maize and wheat.[15] This harvest was later credited by Eliza for the better health of his people.[16] In spite of this they were back on short rations by the time the next year's supplies arrived from San Blas.

Eliza had sent the report of his 1791 voyage to the Viceroy on his return to Nootka and in it he wished to "assure his Excellency that the passage to the (Atlantic) Ocean which foreign nations have sought with such assiduity must be situate at no other place but through this great inlet (of Floridablanca) or else on the opposite side of the continent."

This was good enough for the Viceroy. 1792 was to be the year which would settle the question of the Northwest Passage forever. This would be done by exploring every bay and inlet leading into the strait named for the Greek who used the name of Juan de Fuca.

Interlude

LAS YNSTRUCCIÓNES DEL VIREY

The Viceroy issued instructions for two tasks in 1792. The first task was to send a representative to Nootka to put into effect the rather vague tems of the Nootka Convention. Quadra, by now a *capitan de navio*, the highest naval rank below the various grades of admiral, was chosen as the Commissioner to settle matters with the English at Nootka. George Vancouver had already been dispatched from England to Nootka as His Britannic Majesty's representative.

The Viceroy's instructions to Quadra, dated October 29, 1791, dealt with two subjects: the restoration of lands at Nootka and the compensation to be paid for the losses suffered by Meares and his associates.[1] With respect to the former, the Viceroy was not convinced that there was anything to restore. The Viceroy reminded Quadra that the instructions captured from Meares under which Colnett was operating in 1789 required him to establish a trading post on the coast. The Viceroy took this document as evidence that there had been no settlement at Nootka before Martinez set up the Spanish establecimiento.

The disparity between this viewpoint and that of Vancouver became an important point in the later negotiations. Vancouver considered that Spanish territory did not extend north of San Francisco, although there was nothing in his instructions to that effect.[2]

The Viceroy's instructions to Quadra went on to say that if the English persisted in an unfounded demand for the restoration of property at Nootka, Quadra was to try and work out a provisional arrangement in an amicable way, even to the extent of turning Nootka over to the English if necessary, in which case an alternative outpost in the Strait of Juan de Fuca was to be set up. This would be garrisoned with twenty-five to thirty married men, which was expected to reduce turnover. Apparently twenty-five to thirty married women were expected to settle down happily in makeshift accommodation, surrounded by forest, wet and cold in the winter, among Indians of unknown disposition, cut off from the rest of the world, and exposed to the possibility of starvation if the next year's supply ship did not arrive.

Salutes were to be fired with six cannon on the occasion of the birthdays of the King, the Queen and the Prince of Asturias (the heir to the throne). This was to remind the Indians and any English in the vicinity that the Spaniards were there, and were well armed. The amicable resolution of difficulties apparently had some limits.

There was a limit to the amount of compensation too. Quadra was to work out the amount of damages in detail so as to arrive at a total amount of 653,433 *pesos fuertes* or Spanish dollars. The purpose of an estimate even in those days was to arrive at a desired total.

The Viceroy instructed Quadra to negotiate for a boundary running north from the mouth of the Strait of Juan de Fuca. West of that line, which would include all the known coast north of the Strait, would be a joint British and Spanish trading monopoly, if not actually joint ownership. East of that line would lie the entrance to the Northwest Passage through the Canal de Floridablanca as well as all of the coast between California and the Strait. This would be Spanish territory. A map, a copy of which is in the Archivo de Indias in Seville, was enclosed to illustrate this.[3]

Poor Martinez was to be thrown to the sharks. His lowly rank was to be disclosed (Alferez Martinez had strutted in Commander-in-Chief's feathers) and his actions were to be repudiated.

Finally, Quadra was instructed to collaborate with the English in exploring the coast, to show them the Spanish maps which had been made by Eliza's expedition, and to give them the latitude and longitude of any points which might be dangerous to navigation. He was not to permit the English to copy the maps, nor was he to give them copies.

There is a dream-like quality to many of the instructions issued by Revilla Gigedo. It shows up here in the idea that without reference to Madrid or London, Quadra and Vancouver could negotiate a boundary for Spanish possessions plus a condominium on the coast beyond the boundary. There is also a whiff of the pipe in the thought that the condominium could exclude the Americans from trade on the coast. There is more of such stuff as dreams are made on in the separate instructions issued for the other task to be carried out that year. This was the final search for the Northwest Passage, to be done while Quadra was at Nootka.

The choice of a commander for this expedition fell on Maurelle, the doughty pilot of Quadra's *Sonora* voyage in 1775. In the end Maurelle had to withdraw because of illness and the work was assigned to others but the instructions probably remained more or less the same. Maurelle was to be given the schooner *Mexicana*, recently built in the San Blas dockyard, with supplies for a year.[4] His "ynstrucciónes secretas" dated September 9, 1791 started out very simply.[5] He was to explore the coast in minute detail from San Francisco to 55° North latitude, taking possession of any place worth having and recording his surveys with precision. He was to look out particularly for the river discovered by Martin de Aguilar which had been mislaid somewhere since 1602.

He must first turn his attention to the Strait of Juan de Fuca and the inlets leading into or out of it. He was to determine whether any of these inlets led to Hudson's Bay or Baffin Bay as had been presumed or whether they all led back to the Pacific. This would resolve all doubts and relieve any difficulties that might arise through foreign countries discovering them in the future. The boundary line was to remain unfixed until the return of the schooner.

Having completed this little jaunt to the Atlantic Ocean, or back to the Pacific if the presumed course of the inlets was wrong, Maurelle was to head back to San Francisco, surveying all the way, and send in his report so that the Viceroy could give his orders to the Commissioner at Nootka (Quadra).

After this start on the year's work Maurelle was to head north to 56° then work his way south, still carrying out his meticulous examination until he got back to the Strait of Juan de Fuca. He was to bear in mind that this information was needed immediately so the King could make wise decisions.

Maurelle was empowered to requisition from any Spanish governor, commandant, or ship anything he needed and the latter were to comply without question. Finally, Maurelle was to report directly to the Viceroy and to no one else.   If he succeeded in all this he could expect to be rewarded by the King.

Maurelle then took sick. Since San Blas was notorious for its fever-breeding climate his illness may not have been caused by reading his instructions. There is also the possibility that Malaspina, who was very influential, wanted his own men on the voyage and that the illness was a diplomatic one. Apparently Maurelle was well enough to take *Mexicana* from San Blas to Acapulco at the end of December.[6]

Whatever the reason, Maurelle's replacement leads him out of our story.

7

LAS GOLETAS

In October 1791 Malaspina arrived back in Acapulco from his tour to Alaska.[1] All the officers chosen by the Viceroy for the exploration of the Strait of Juan de Fuca were drawn from Malaspina's ships.

The *goleta* or schooner *Sutil*, a sister ship of *Mexicana* which had been assigned to Maurelle, was launched in November and both these little ships were to go to the Strait.[2] *Sutil* was commanded by Dionisio Alcalá Galiano; *Mexicana* by Cayetano Valdés. As the senior of the two officers Galiano was in charge of the expedition. Both of these officers had left Spain with Malaspina in 1789, but Galiano had spent the year 1791 in Mexico, bringing the expedition's astronomical calculations and maps up to date.[3] Thus he missed the trip to Alaska.

The goletas, said the San Blas dockyard officials to the Viceroy, were better suited to work than any others available.[4] They were the most seaworthy of the available ships, and their shallow draft made them both suitable for exploring shallow channels and easy to handle under sail or oars. The facilities at Acapulco, including the shipwrights and caulkers in the crew of Malaspina's ships, were better than those at San Blas (said the dockyard) so the schooners would be sent there for fitting out, with all materials and equipment needed for the purpose on board. This was to include materials for altering the rig if this proved necessary. The Viceroy approved all this, and it appears that at least one of the assigned officers went to San Blas to bring the schooners down the coast to Acapulco.

These "most seaworthy" schooners were 50 feet 3 inches in length and had a beam of 13 feet 3 inches. These measurements are in Spanish feet, which were equal to 28 centimetres or about eleven English inches. Their burden was 45 tons compared to 340 tons for Vancouver's *Discovery*.[5] About half of the schooners' weight would have been stone or gravel ballast, which would take up quite a lot of the space in the hold. There was no timber, tar, oakum, or tools aboard. *"Las atenciones del Departmento habian sedo muy superiores a los medios"*: the Department's solicitude had been much better than its resources.

The officers had a cabin in the poop which Vancouver said was just large enough to accommodate a table at which four could sit in some discomfort. The seamen would just have to find a place to sleep in the hold. In Vancouver's opinion *Sutil* and *Mexicana* were "the most unfit and ill-calculated vessels that could be imagined for such an expedition."[6]

We are told nothing about cooking arrangements, but it was typical of that period that there would have been a brick hearth somewhere on which a wood fire could be lit in good weather. In bad weather the diet would be mostly ship's biscuit and water, with wine or an occasional dash of brandy for the officers.

The goletas were provided with oars and could be rowed if the wind failed. This was done many times in navigating the inlets and channels but when entering or leaving a harbour they sometimes launched a boat and towed the ship. The leadsman could then take soundings ahead, which reduced the chance of grounding. From boats, or from the ship itself, sounding was done with a long line with a lead weight on the end. A lump of tallow was stuck to the bottom of the lead and the leadsman would report not only the depth but the nature of the bottom, reporting "four fathoms sand,""six fathoms black mud," and so on. I am inferring the type of equipment, but soundings are reported in this way in the *Relación*. If nothing stuck to the tallow they called the bottom "rock" and looked for another place to anchor.

On the way from San Blas to Acapulco the bread had been ruined by water which leaked into the store rooms. The vegetables, which the commanders knew to be a necessity to avoid scurvy, were also damaged. Furthermore, there was not enough room below to store the required supplies, nor enough casks to store the needed fresh water. Previous voyages, from Perez on, had shown that it was not possible to beat up the California coast against the prevailing wind and put in to replenish water supplies from time to time. Then as now, a sailing vessel heading north from Acapulco must put to sea, pick up the northeast trades, work northwards and finally run down its eastings when far enough north to pick up the westerlies of the temperate zone. Pilot charts showed such a route until 1950, just as described by the narrator of the *Relación*.

The schooners also had shown a marked lack of strength and stability on the short voyage from San Blas to Acapulco and they leaked abominably. To crown all, the "goletas" or "schooners" weren't even that. Their rig was a mixture of schooner and brigantine.

"We" as the narrator calls the officers of the expedition, or sometimes the ship's company, or occasionally the ships themselves, thought this over for a while. Since personal pronouns are not used much in Spanish and not at all in the *Relación*, I have a bit of a problem sometimes following the meaning. In this passage it was not too difficult to deduce that *"pensamos"* means "we (i.e. the officers) thought" ... and so on.

A plan to remedy the defects was developed and submitted to the Viceroy for approval. There was no apparent advantage to the mixed rig, but by switching spars, sails, and rigging between the ships, *Sutil* could be converted to a brigantine and *Mexicana* to a schooner. When Vancouver later described *Sutil* as a brig he was just using an abbreviation for "brigantine."[7] The distinction between brig and brigantine came in the nineteenth century.

To increase the space in the hold, the main deck would be raised thirteen inches to the level of the top of the well deck. Interior partitioning would be removed and replaced with two bulkheads, providing a storeroom forward and another aft for cargo and provisions. Additional water casks were also to be made. To restore the strength lost by the structural changes, *embonos* two feet deep and three inches thick, increased to four inches amidships, would be fitted. There are several possible meanings for "embono" but in the context I think it was probably a strake run along the side of the ship partly above the deck line to stiffen her and replace the bulwarks lost when the well deck was taken into the hold. The Viceroy, who seems to have been good at approving, gave his consent.

Consent did not supply tools, materials, or tradesmen. There was one carpenter and one caulker in the crews of the schooners, both third class ratings. A few town carpenters and some Filipinos from another ship were recruited and Galiano's men rounded up the only three pit saws in Acapulco to cut fresh cedar logs into planks. Using the old naval method of "steal what you can't scrounge" they set to work. The essential parts of the work got done, including the lining of a locker with pitch, canvas and sheets of tin to protect the new bread supply and the new vegetables, which were of the best quality.

The shore commandant at Acapulco then made a gesture. There was a *sangrador* among a group of prisoners under sentence of transportation to the Philippines and this "leech" was transferred to *Mexicana* along with a book on medicine.

The narrative pays due tribute to the Viceroy's indefatigable energy and his devotion to the service of the King. The lapse of two centuries makes it difficult to judge whether this was sincere, sycophantic, or ironic.

Finally on March 8, 1792 all was ready. The crew spent the morning stowing away the last of the stores but there was a flat calm and all they could do was wait for a breeze.

Interlude

OFICIALES Y TRIPULACIÓN

In talking about officers and crew, we should start with Malaspina. Galiano, Valdés and the rest had been under his command since 1789, and as I have said, I suspect he chose them for the expedition to the Strait of Juan de Fuca. Malaspina was a Parmesan. At the time Parma was a duchy under the suzerainty of Spain, ruled by the brother of Carlos III in Malaspina's younger days. His native language was Italian, but Italy as a country did not then exist. He was always considered an outsider in court circles in Spain. His voyage, which did not in the end take him all the way around the world, lasted until 1794.

On his return to Spain he fell afoul of Manuel Godoy, reputedly the Queen's lover. Since Godoy was also Prime Minister this led to Malaspina being locked up for eight years. Opinion seems to be divided on whether the quarrel was due to Malaspina's advanced ideas, such as self government for the colonies, or whether it was because the Queen got too much enjoyment out of the private drawing lessons given to her by Malaspina. There was the usual business of an incriminating letter which may have been planted by one of the ladies in waiting who was under Godoy's influence.[1] The account of Malaspina's voyage was locked up for ninety years, and his name was not even mentioned in references to his voyage. He was referred to occasionally as El Comandante but more often the names of his ships were used instead.

Our chief interest is in his officers. There were Dionisio Alcalá Galiano and Cayetano Valdés, both frigate captains, and Lieutenants Secundino Salamanca and Juan Vernaci, who were the pilots of the two ships. There was also a man named Joseph Cardero who was not an officer but who is accorded the honorific prefix of "Don" in the narrative. He had been assigned to the position of *dibuxante* during Malaspina's voyage.[2] The primary job of the dibuxante was the preparation of maps, but often he was also an artist.

Malaspina left to continue his voyage across the Pacific and these five were detached to take *Sutil* and *Mexicana* to the northern coast and

57

settle the Northwest Passage question. In addition to the officers and Cardero, there were seventeen men in each ship. The seamen are nameless, and beyond some remarks about how hard they had to work we know nothing about them. We are told there were three petty officers, seven gunners, six sailors, and a soldier. There was also a servant or page in each ship, but these were not counted as members of the crew.[3] We can guess at their labours in making and handing sail or raising half a ton of anchor and cable when the ships anchored out in thirty fathoms or more. We are told that with the exception of one sick man exchanged ashore at Nootka they all returned to San Blas in good health, which was a marked improvement over all the earlier expeditions.

We don't know much more about the lieutenants. They appear on our stage as junior officers with Malaspina, they pilot Galiano's ships, they explore the inlets in launches, then they return to San Blas and are lost from sight.

Galiano is a little clearer. He was born in Cabra in Córdoba province in 1760[4] and entered the navy at fifteen, which the editor of the *Enciclopedia General del Mar* thought was an early age, although the English were taking midshipmen younger than that. The next year he was in action against the Portuguese and only a few years later began to be recognized as a hydrographer. From about 1783 until after his voyage in *Sutil* his main activity was exploration and mapping.

Somewhere along the line he married, and there was a son who was offered a commission in the navy. Galiano senior declined this honour because he had other plans for the lad. The "other plans" are not specified, but later his son's *Memorias* became the source of the information in the *Enciclopedia*.

We will see later that Galiano and his fellow officers became friends of the English officers Vancouver and Broughton, but his country was at war with England through much of his naval career. Spain was still at war with England in 1805 when Galiano led his squadron to sea and ran into a large enemy force. In the battle Galiano was wounded and finally "an English ball of medium calibre shattered his head, taking his life." He fell on October 21, and the cape nearby was called Trafalgar.

Valdés was a few years younger. He was born in 1767 and was in action against the English at the age of fifteen. He escaped the battle of Trafalgar with a wound and then we lose sight of him for a while. In 1823 he was exiled from Spain and had to live in England for ten years. Perhaps it was because his family were involved in the disorderly politics of the time. He had an uncle or brother who was navy minister at the time of his voyage with Galiano. He weathered this and returned to Spain to end his days as a lieutenant general in the Spanish service.[5]

Cardero was born in 1766.[6] His name appears in the *Relación* only once, in the crew list when the goletas left Acapulco. One historian did not think he was with Malaspina at all.[7] He is not listed in the complement of Malaspina's officers, nor is he mentioned by Malaspina as being among those detached at Acapulco.[8] It appears that he was a member of the crew. He served as artist after Malaspina's official artist had been sent home from Lima, a post he obtained because Valdés was impressed with his abilities.[9] There is even some argument as to whether he drew some of the sketches attributed to him; it is known that quite often one artist would complete or copy another one's sketch.[10] Cardero returned to Spain with Valdés after the 1792 voyage and joined Valdés on a voyage to Cartagena in 1794. In 1795 he and his family moved to Cadiz where he worked on the maps of the Galiano Voyage. He was a "ship's accountant" at that time. His name appears on the Navy List for the first time in 1797 and by 1808 he was a second officer. His name disappears from the Navy List after 1810 because of death or resignation from the service.

This is all we know of the thirty-nine men (and two servants) waiting in Acapulco for a wind to take *Sutil* and *Mexicana* off on their voyage.

8

THE VOYAGE TO
NOOTKA

Early in the afternoon the breeze came and they were able to weigh anchor and make sail. Soon after clearing Acapulco harbour they had to head south. Yes, south. The wind was in the west and the best the ships could do on the other tack would have been a little west of north, which would run them into the coast. Eighteenth-century ships could make very little progress to windward. The commanders soon realized there was another limitation. In any sort of a breeze they would have to shorten sail. So much for the handiest and most seaworthy ships in the Department of San Blas. Ten days later they had lost five degrees of northing and gained less than three degrees of west latitude. To their disgust, even with moderate westerlies the best they could do "on the wind" was three knots.

At last the wind veered, and by crowding on all the sail they could carry they gained latitude on northerly and north easterly winds. By the 29th of March (three weeks out) they were back in the latitude of Acapulco and had gained fifteen degrees to the west. Progress westward had averaged forty miles per day and they were hardly nearer to the Strait of Juan de Fuca than when they started. This was about half the rate of progress of "las Corbetas" the year before, when winds were not any more favourable. "Las Corbetas" were *Descubierta* and *Atrevida* and Malaspina had been the leader, but of course by the time the *Relación* was published Malaspina was, in Geoge Orwell's phrase, an unperson.

The next recorded event was the breaking of the barometer, which was secured to the shrouds for want of a better place to put it. The ingenuity of Spanish seamen was not limited to raising decks and waterproofing bread lockers. This is about as ingenious an excuse for damage to expensive equipment as any used by navy men in the Second World War.

Early in April things picked up a bit. The winds were now easterly to south easterly and some measurements of lunar distances were obtained to check the chronometers, a matter of some concern since the ships made so much leeway that they seldom knew the direction in which they were travelling. On the fourteenth, both ships were roaring along on a broad reach trying to make up for lost time by flying everything but the cook's apron or, in the more sedate phrase of the *Relación*, sailing with studding sails set when *Mexicana's* mainmast broke six and a half feet below the topmast. Sailors never seem to learn that time lost is lost forever and that each watch must be sailed to its own weather. Galiano let fly *Sutil's* topsails and, having ascertained that there were no injuries on *Mexicana* and no damage other than the broken mast, told Valdés to steer the best course he could. *Sutil* would then move ahead and keep station on *Mexicana*, and they would go to Nootka for repairs.

Night fell before the wreckage could be cleared away and a strong westerly blew up, with very rough seas. *Mexicana* could keep control only by running off before the wind, losing the precious westing they still needed. Galiano took station ahead and sailed under foresails only to maintain contact. He promised to send over a carpenter as soon as a boat could be launched, although Valdés said he could make it to Nootka. For three days it blew and the best *Mexicana* could do was to sail ten points off the wind, which gained a little to the north at the expense of being pressed in towards the coast. Then the sea flattened out and the carpenter was able to get across to *Mexicana* and help set up a jury rig. Using *Mexicana's* oars as a derrick to raise a new mast, and with the aid of a spare yard passed over from *Sutil*, the crew finally got the jury rig set up and the ships were under way a week after the dismasting. They tried to make way to the northwest but adverse winds and currents set them in towards the coast and they ended up only twenty leagues from the land in 42° North latitude, still nearly five hundred miles from Nootka.

Sailors are slow to learn another maxim: whatever the weather may be, it's going to change. Now an easterly wind got up and the ships stood out to sea. Pilots with much experience in those waters had advised them to keep to a longitude at least 33° west of Acapulco until they reached the latitude of Nootka and picked up the north-west wind. Maurelle wrote the first sailing directions for voyaging north from California[1] although there may have been later ones to which the narrator is referring. The wind came up from the south so they forgot this advice and the south wind blew them gently into Nootka. "If we hadn't lost the mast because of our anxiety to reach Juan de Fuca," said the narrator, "we would never have found out how wrong those *maldi-*

ción cancelada pilots were." The original sentence is more polished and polite but I think my translation is what he meant.

The narrative tells one how to make a neat and seamanlike approach to Nootka on a westerly. You keep close in to the islands which close off the anchorage, within a musket shot in fact, and just as you reach the entrance you let go all sails. If the vessel has fine lines she will just have way enough to come up to the best anchorage. If she is bulky, you need a little wind on the hull to make it all the way, but if you fall a little short there is still good anchorage.

The evidence of the text suggests to a historiographer that the narrator was not *Sutil's* pilot, because what actually happened was that she grounded outside and both ships were towed into the harbour by boats sent out from the *establecimiento*.

This carving of the tiny man in a mussel shell is a symbol of the Indian legend of the creation of man. It lay buried for five hundred years in the mud which engulfed a village at the place now known as Ozette, in the State of Washington. The legend is still intact in the oral history of the natives of the outer coast, from the north end of Vancouver Island to Cape Flattery. Courtesy Makah Cultural and Research Center.

Interlude

OZETTE

When the schooners arrived at Nootka, Chief Maquinna was delighted to see his friends Valdés, Vernaci, and Salamanca. Galiano was making his first voyage to Nootka and Cardero is not mentioned. Quadra had been there two weeks and Maquinna had already made friends with him, dining "close to" his table. Maquinna used a knife and fork in the European manner and relied on his friends to tell him when he had drunk enough "Spanish water" or wine. He complained about the conduct of other foreigners and denied that he had ever sold any land to Meares. He was happy to receive gifts from his Spanish friends and only too glad to make gifts to them, but as a chief he did not engage in personal trading.

This is all reported by a Spanish narrator. We must remember that the instructions to Spanish commanders usually, if not always, emphasized the importance of friendly relations with the native people. Under these circumstances it is not to be expected that an official Spanish account would deride or disparage Maquinna or his people.

Nevertheless, there were many remarks in the journals of English and American traders on the friendship between the Spaniards and the Indians, and on the ability of the Spaniards to speak the native languages. Some of these comments were admiring, some were jealous but, except for some doubtful statements by Meares and Colnett, they all agreed that the Spaniards, particularly Quadra, were great friends of the Indian chiefs.

Of course we do not have Maquinna's views. We see him only through the eyes and pens of others. He had dealings with most of the explorers and traders who had been on the Coast since 1774, so we have many accounts of him. He seems to have been inclined to play along with any white man who showed up, or at least with the one who had the upper hand at the time. When there was trouble among the Europeans, as happened between Martinez and Colnett, Maquinna simply gathered up his people and left, although he always came back again when the fuss died down.

What is true of Maquinna is true of his people. All we know of them is what the English, American or Spanish eyes saw and what their pens wrote down. Apart from oral tradition, this is all that Maquinna's own descendants know. The question remains: How good were those eyes? How faithful were those pens?

I began to feel some confidence in the Spanish accounts, not because of anything that happened at Nootka but because of a natural disaster which had happened three centuries earlier on the coast of the present State of Washington, at a place now called the Ozette Indian Reservation.

Some time in the fifteenth century a landslide engulfed some of the houses in a village at Ozette, smothering them in dense mud. Part of this mud deposit was eroded away by the sea in 1970 and, at the invitation of the Makah Tribal Council, the archaeologists from Washington State University went to work. Because the mud excluded oxygen, articles made of wood and of cedar bark, roots, and grasses were recovered, as well as articles made of bone, antler, shell, and stone. The wreckage of the houses was still in place. Thousands of artifacts were recovered, and a selection of these is on display in the museum of the Makah Cultural and Research Centre at Neah Bay. You may go and see them as I did, so I am only going to mention the items which are duplicated in the Spanish descriptions of Nootka and of other villages.

The houses were built of cedar. Posts for supporting the roof beams were logs set vertically into the ground, notched at the top for the beams. Logs running the length of the house served as beams. The planks of the roof were not attached to the beams. They could be moved aside to let in air or to let out smoke. The walls were made of planks, lashed to vertical poles on both sides to form a wall panel. Planks were made by splitting cedar logs with yew or spruce wedges, and some of them bear incised designs of animals and birds. The panels were lashed to the corner posts, using cedar or spruce fibre.

Low platforms covered with mats were used for sleeping. The Indians' possessions were stored in bentwood boxes or woven baskets. Dog hair was spun and woven into capes or blankets combined with cedar bark. Wooden boxes were used for boiling food, usually fish, which was put into the box with water. Rocks heated by the fire were dropped into the water using a pair of wooden tongs. Tongs with charred ends and rocks splintered by dropping them into cold water can be seen at the museum. In the houses, wooden rods were hung horizontally below the roof beams, and it is presumed these were used for hanging dried fish.

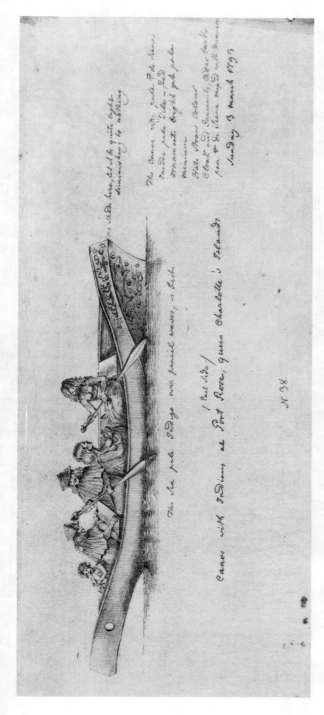

A Haida woman's canoe at Rose Harbour in the Queen Charlotte or Haida Islands. The drawing was made in 1793 by Sigismund Bacstrom, but there was probably little change from 1774 when Perez became the first European to make contact with the Indians of the Pacific Northwest, not far from the spot where this drawing was made. Courtesy British Columbia Provincial Archives, from an original drawing in their collection.

Above and opposite: The Spanish flag flies over the Canadian west coast, at the fort which guards the entrance to Nootka Sound. The frigate was probably Eliza's Concepción which was at the "Cala de los Amigos" (Friendly Cove) for two years. The decks are covered and the upper masts and rigging have been sent down. Just behind the tallest mast is the observatory tent where latitude and longitude were observed. This engraving was made from a Cardero drawing for the 1802 publication of the Relación of Galiano's voyage. It represents the scene as it appeared in 1791, before the two storey Commandant's house was built. Courtesy Vancouver Public Library.

The great wrestling game was played during the celebration of the onset of puberty in Maquinna's daughter. At the right some Spanish sailors are stripping to join the game. Courtesy Vancouver Public Library.

Sutil leads the way, flying Galiano's pennant at the mainmast. Mexicana follows, spilling the wind from her sails to slow the ship. The Indians in the canoe closest to the ship are shown in the standard pose depicted in scenes from California to Alaska. The artist may have drawn on his imagination in sketching the canoe and its occupants. The canoe with the fish spear looks more authentic. This picture was drawn by Cardero among the islands to the east of the San Juans, which appear on the 1791 map. The mountain is Mount Baker. Courtesy Museo Naval de Madrid.

Portrait of Don Estevan Jose Martinez, Fernando Martinez de la Sierra, Frigate Lieutenant of the Royal Armada, Commander of various expeditions on the Northwest Coast of America, first Spanish discoverer of that coast and of the Russian establishments, head of the expedition to San Lorenzo de Nuca, born in Seville the 9th of December, 1742. Courtesy Museo Naval de Madrid.

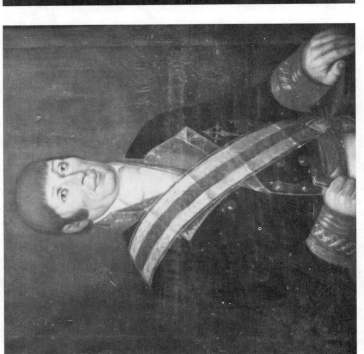

His Excellency Francisco Antonio Mourelle (Maurelle) General Commander in 1819 of the Grand Expedition of the Ultramar. The first voyager to explore to the 62nd parallel of North latitude; Discoverer of the Vavao group (Tonga) and other islands of Oceania. Born 1754 and died 1825. Courtesy Museo Naval de Madrid.

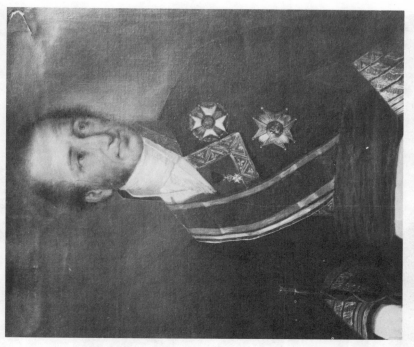

Cayetano Valdés, who accompanied Alcalá Galiano in Command of Mexicana. Courtesy Museo Naval de Madrid.

Dionisio Alcalá Galiano, commandant of the 1792 exploration of the waters to the east of present day Vancouver Island. His ship was Sutil. Courtesy Museo Naval de Madrid.

On March 17, 1984 King Juan Carlos and Queen Sofia of Spain unveiled a bronze bust of Bodega y Quadra in a park in Victoria, British Columbia. Mayor Peter Pollen is with them, wearing his chain of office. This picture is included because no authentic portrait of the great Spanish naval captain is known to exist. Courtesy John McKay.

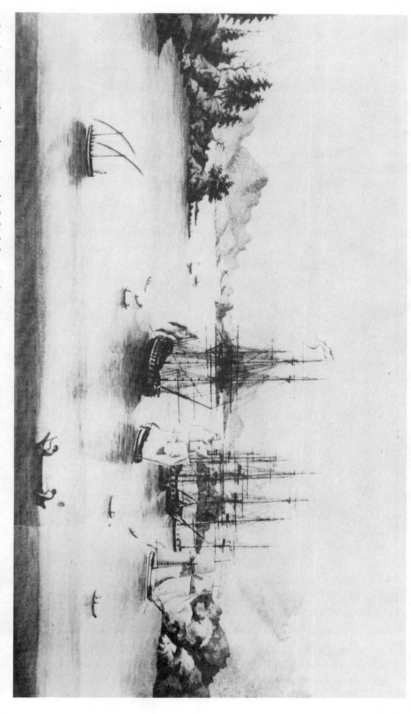

This drawing of the anchorage at the Cala de los Amigos is a composite. Sutil and Mexicana are far too small in relation to the size of the frigates. They are shown with all plain sail set although anchored fore and aft. The other ships probably represent Santa Gertrudis on the left, Aranzazu and Concepción in the centre, and the schooner Activa behind them. Courtesy Ministerio de Asuntos Exteriores, Madrid.

73

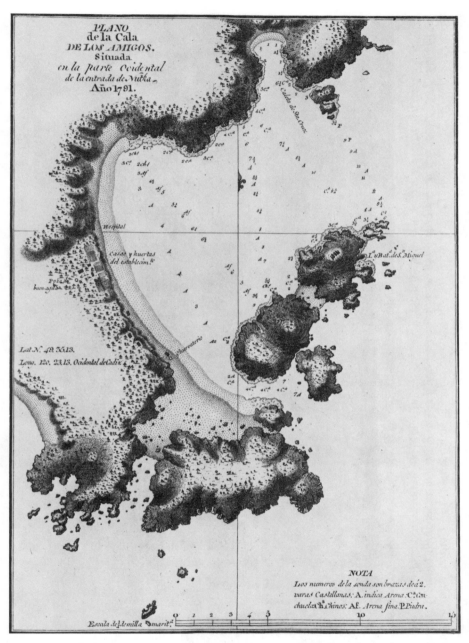

The Spanish map of the Cala de los Amigos *or Friendly Cove. The hospital, the observatory, and the houses and gardens of the* establecimiento *with the well behind them are shown. Courtesy Vancouver Public Library.*

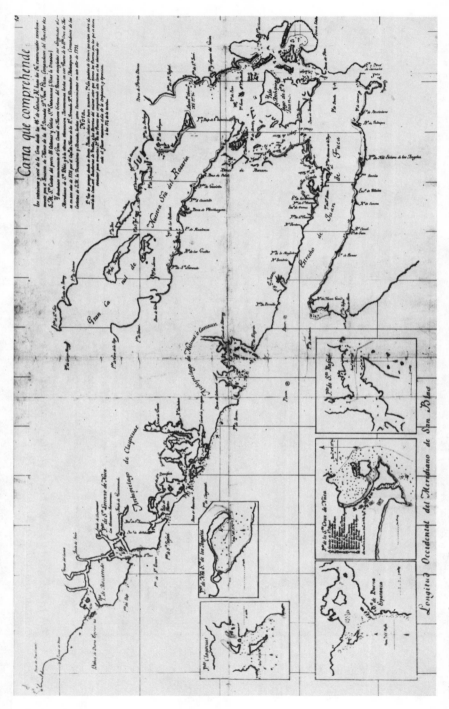

The 1791 Spanish map of the Strait of Juan de Fuca and the Gran Canal de Nuestra Señora del Rosario, later renamed the Gulf of Georgia, now called the Strait of Georgia by purists. Courtesy Museo Naval de Madrid.

The first page of the Nootka vocabulary as recorded by Moziño in his Noticias de Nutka. There are a number of manuscript copies of his work. This one is from Tomo 558. Courtesy Archivo General de la Nación.

This well known engraving of the interior of an Indian house was made from a drawing by John Webber, who was with Captain Cook when he visited Nootka on his way to the Bering Strait in 1778. It shows many details corresponding to the descriptions in Moziño's Noticias de Nutka. Courtesy British Columbia Provincial Archives.

Tetacus (opposite) was the chief who travelled from Nuñez Gaona to Cordoba with Valdés. His wives, one of whom was Maria (above), followed by canoe. There is a strong resemblance between Tetacus's portrait and that of Maquinna (page 6). The artist Cardero drew the same European features for most of his portraits of Indian men. Courtesy Vancouver Public Library.

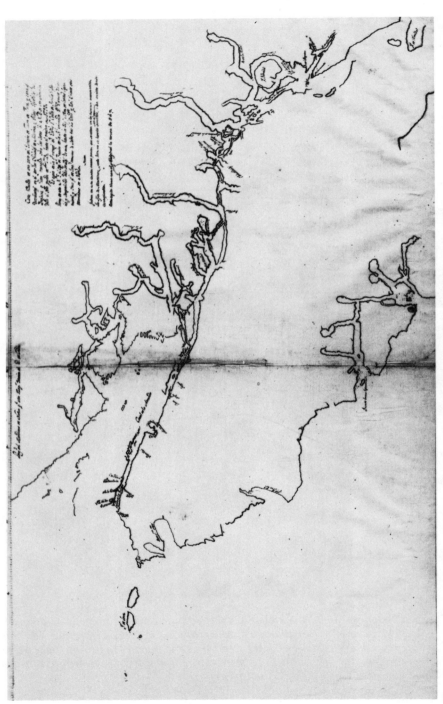

Galiano's map of the "Narrow Waters" to the north of present day Vancouver Island. Courtesy Museo Naval de Madrid.

Clothing was recovered from the mud at Ozette, including capes of cedar bark and hats woven from roots and grasses. The hats are conical and are woven closely enough to be waterproof. Some of them have a woven knob on top, others are flat-topped.

In the Makah Museum, there is a herring rake with bone teeth set in its edge, fishing lines made of cedar bark, and cedar-root fishing nets for small fish. Whaling harpoons have heavy yew-wood shafts with heads made of antler or mussel shell. A two-strand cedar bark rope is tied at one end to the harpoon head and at the other to a float. The shaft has a pointed end fitted into the head, so that the shaft can be recovered, leaving the head embedded in the whale. Floats are shown in the museum, made by skinning a seal without slitting the hide and plugging the flipper and neck openings, but these are replicas of floats used in the early years of the twentieth century, since no animal tissue other than bones or antlers was preserved by the mud.

Canoes were dugouts made of cedar, ranging in size from a one man (or one woman) canoe up to the big whaling canoes which held six or eight men and all their equipment.

Copper and iron were both in use in small amounts at the fifteenth-century Ozette village. Copper was used mostly for small ornamental pieces, but the remains of several iron knives were found during the excavation. All that remained of one large knife was the rust stain on the surrounding mud.[1]

These are only a few of the artifacts displayed at the Makah Museum, which in turn are only a few of the artifacts found at Ozette. In most cases they match closely the descriptions and sketches given to us by the Spaniards. Both Perez and Maurelle saw iron knives, and evidently iron had been in use on the coast three centuries earlier. The similarities are not only in canoes, houses, and tools, but also in a tiny carving depicting the origin of man, a legend I will narrate in the next chapter.

To the extent one can judge from physical objects, and it is limited, the Spanish accounts of Indian life are confirmed by the findings at Ozette.

9

THE NATIVE PEOPLE

Quadra brought a scientist with him to Nootka. Don Joseph Mariano Moziño Suarez was a creole who had studied theology, ethics and mathematics in Mexican universities before graduating in medicine. He had been trained as a naturalist by the Director of the Royal Scientific Expedition which was in New Spain from 1787 to 1803.[1] Moziño had a botanist and an artist with him, and he stayed at Nootka for the five months Quadra was there. His *Noticias de Nutka* give the best surviving account of the Indians of that vicinity as they were in 1792.[2] The narrator of Galiano's voyage quoted Moziño's work in his description of Indian life.

Moziño was not the first European to describe the Nootka Indians. They had been in contact with Europeans and Americans for some years. James Cook (1778) and some of his officers wrote accounts of Indian life. As well, Alexander Walker studied them closely when he visited Nootka in 1785 in the trading ship *Experiment*.[3] Martinez even claimed that Maquinna recognized him from his voyage with Perez in 1774. These first visits had little permanent impact on Indian life, but from 1785 on most of the traders had called at Nootka, so European materials, implements, and even weapons were used to some extent by the Indians. By the time Moziño arrived in 1792 Eliza's people had been living at Nootka for two years. Indian ways had been adjusted to the new supply of materials (particularly iron and copper) brought by the Europeans. Although these materials had altered aboriginal life to some extent, the period of Spanish residence gave Moziño an excellent base from which to start his observations. Moziño's account of the native people is combined here with some information from Caamaño's journal kept during his stay at Nootka in 1790-91.[4] Moziño may not have seen this. I will also repeat some descriptions in the preceding interlude to show the similarities between the Spanish accounts and the artifacts which had been buried three centuries earlier at Ozette.

Moziño describes the people as being short and broad-shouldered, with feet turned inward and legs dwarfed which he said probably resulted from long hours in canoes, so that both men and women had difficulty in walking. "Canoe Indians" of this physical type were seen as late as the early 1900s but with the use of other means of transport and in some cases the admixture of European genes the physique of modern Indians has changed in this respect. Moziño comments on the flattened noses and broad nostrils and the high wide-set cheekbones, which he attributes to the habit of binding the heads of infants. There are many reports of this practice. Caamaño reported it, and also that of binding the infant's body in a cradle for eighteen months. Binding may have affected the shape of the head, but I think some of my acquaintances among the Coast Indians would recognize themselves in Moziño's description of facial configuration.

Curiously, this head and face shape is not evident in most of the portrait drawings of Indians made by a number of European artists. Perhaps they unconsciously drew a European head when they set out to draw a portrait of an Indian.

These people covered the entire body with a layer of grease or whale oil smeared over with red clay or charcoal or sometimes with the down or feathers of birds. This covering was so heavy that Moziño was unable to discern skin colour, but assumed from the colour of the children, that it was not as dark as that of the Mexicans. He observed hair colour ranging from light brown to black, but does not seem to consider that hair too could have been anointed with some coloured mixture.

The only clothing of the men was a conical hat woven from grass and a square cape woven from cedar bark fibre and animal hair, which was discarded when the weather did not require its use. The women wore the same type of cape, supplemented by a fringed cloth hanging from a belt and an inner cape covering the breasts. This apparel seems to have stayed in place while the Spaniards were around. The Indians had no footwear. This is why, when the first Europeans came to Nootka, it was thought that they had wooden feet.[5]

Chiefs wore a more elaborate cape of softened deerskin or sea otter fur, and Maquinna had a cape of marten fur which was so finely made that the seams could only be seen on the reverse side. In cold weather a fur cape would be worn with the fur side next to the body for additional warmth.

The hats of commoners were plain, but the chiefs decorated theirs with whale hunting scenes and added the small onion-shaped finial on top which we think of as the "Maquinna hat." Hats were woven over a mandrel, using reeds or the rushes we call cattails, with a binding thread made by stripping fibres from the shaft of a birds's feather. The hats recovered at Ozette used cedar bark for binding, and Kevin Neary of the

Ethnology Division of the British Columbia Provincial Museum has told me that although eighteen "Maquinna" hats have been recovered none of them used feather shafts.

Moziño said that the houses reflected poverty and were very dirty and untidy.[6] Caamaño, whose journal was not an official report, went further. He said that large groups of people lived together in one house and, between the whale oil with which they anointed themselves and the fact that they "did necessities" indoors, the stench was unimaginable. This is confirmed by Moziño who said fish were cleaned and shellfish extracted from their shells inside the house, and much of the residue stayed where it fell.

As at Ozette, the houses were made of wood, probably red cedar. The roof beams, each a single log running the length of the house were supported by posts made of tree trunks, with notches at the top for the beams. Moziño says pitched roofs were used, with the posts at the sides of the house being much shorter than the central ones. Most of the drawings of Indian houses at Nootka show almost flat roofs, like the houses at Ozette. Perhaps by 1792 the Indians had copied Spanish designs to the extent of using pitched roofs. Apparently axes and saws had not yet found their way into Indian tool chests, because Moziño says that the only way they could fell a tree was by burning it away at the base. Other visitors have said that the Indians used adzes and chisels to cut away the base of a tree.[7] As at Ozette three hundred years earlier, planks for the walls and roof were made by splitting logs with wooden wedges. Roof planks were left loose, and could be moved aside to admit air and light and to provide an outlet for smoke. The wall planks were lashed to vertical wales on both sides and also lashed to the corner posts. Lashings were made from bark fibre or roots.

Some of the house posts were carved with "grotesque" human faces (sketches by artists sometimes show animal heads) but this is the only mention of anything resembling a totem pole as we would know it, nor do any of the many drawings made by artists show a totem pole. Caamaño said that carved faces, which he too described as "grotesque" were placed high up on trees, and that these were portraits of dead chiefs. I infer that these were objects hung in trees rather than carved on them, but his wording is not entirely clear.

Moziño at first supposed that these carvings had some spiritual significance but was told by the Indians that they were only decorations. James Cook had made a similar observation during his voyage. Cook said that for "a small matter of brass or iron he could have purchased all of the gods in the place."[8]

Inside the houses were many boxes used to store the property of the people, particularly capes and masks used for dancing. Moziño's description of these boxes says they were made of separate pieces of wood, fitted together in the same way as those made by Spanish artisans. This is the first item I have noticed that is not confirmed by the objects recovered at Ozette, where boxes were made of a plank scarfed and bent to form a square, with the open edge held together with dowels.

Around the walls were sleeping platforms covered with mats, separated by low partitions. Strings of *sardinas* and other dried fish hung below the roof beams. It is not certain what species the sardinias were. They may have been small perch or possibly herrings. Bladders full of whale oil hung from the walls.

There were few kitchen utensils. They had some cauldrons used for boiling fish by partly filling them with fish and water and dropping in stones heated in the fire, using a pair of wooden tongs.

Fish were also roasted in front of a fire or in the embers. It is not clear whether the containers used for boiling fish were wooden or metal pails acquired by trade or whether they were manufactured by the Indians from wood or reeds, although Moziño did say that kitchen utensils were made of wood.

The sea was the main source of food. Whales were hunted from small canoes using a harpoon with a detachable head. The harpoon was driven with great strength into the body of the whale. The haft was recovered by means of an attached line. Another line attached the head of the harpoon to an inflated bladder; this float marked the position of the animal and was followed until the whale died. It was then towed ashore and the oil was recovered and stored for later use. Moziño does not describe the process of extracting the oil. Whale meat was distributed to everyone, but there is no mention of any attempt to cure the meat.

A French explorer named Etienne Marchand, who had anchored off Barkley Sound in 1791 gave a somewhat different version of the whale hunt.[9] He said five canoes about thirty to thirty-five feet long would line up, each carrying six men. They carried strong stabbing lances and lighter harpoons each attached to a leather bottle by a rope which was two to two and one-half inches in circumference. The whale was stabbed in a vital spot by the heavy lance and the lighter harpoons with the attached floats were stuck into the whale as markers. This corresponds more closely with the equipment recovered at Ozette than does Moziño's account. Mr. Neary and some other ethnologists think that both Moziño and Marchand made some mistakes in the description of the whale hunt.

Fishhooks used for smaller fish were iron ones acquired in trade, although bone and horn points, probably originally attached to wooden hooks, have been recovered by archaeologists at Nootka.[10] Fish nets were small and used only for catching small fish. Sardinias were also caught by assembling canoes across the mouth of a small cove and driving the fish shoreward by agitating long poles in the water. The fish were then baled out with baskets or nets, or impaled on the teeth of a rake. The rake was a long flat board with bone teeth fitted along the edge of it. It was used for any small fish found in schools.

Both fish and fish eggs were smoked for later use. Herring spawn was gathered by lowering a fence of green cedar boughs into the water at the right time and place, according to Caamaño. I have seen this method used to gather herring eggs and I am told by Mr. Neary that this is still done. Whale oil or sardinia oil was mixed with the cooked food, and deer meat or the flesh of sea birds was eaten in addition to fish. In season berries and fresh shoots or roots of young plants were added to the diet. Bread and sweets introduced by the Europeans were popular but milk, butter and cheese were not. Olive oil was poor stuff compared to the aromatic fish oils to which the Indians were accustomed. However, the Spanish food most relished by the Indians was a plate of beans. One of Maquinna's henchmen even adopted the name *Frijoles*.

Thus far Moziño's discourse on the Indians at Nootka is largely a description of tangible objects or events, which an observer can see and record. To go beyond a simple description, the observer has to talk to the Indians, ask them questions, and understand their answers. How well did the Spaniards, including Moziño, understand what the Indians were saying? How well did the Indians understand the Spaniards?

We have no evidence on the latter question and incomplete evidence on the former. There is a "Nootka" word list in Moziño's *Noticias*. This list is much the same as the one in Quadra's journal,[11] with some minor phonetic changes and some alternate Indian words for Spanish terms. I have seen a manuscript copy of Quadra's journal and discovered a few discrepancies which have crept into the best known English translation of Moziño's account at some stage in its transcription from the original eighteenth-century script.[12]

The provenance of Moziño's word list is not altogether clear. We know that in 1789 Joseph Ingraham, mate of the American trader *Lady Washington*, gave Martinez a word list he had compiled in English, which appeared in Spanish in Martinez' diary.[13] The Martinez word list matches Moziño's quite well, after allowing for transcription errors. Even James Cook had compiled a word list during a four-week stay at a nearby cove, and it has a number of similarities with the later lists.[14] Consistency is not the same thing as validity, and it is possible that the consistency between these lists could indicate nothing more than a copying of earlier lists by later writers.

I have had the advantage of reviewing the word lists with Barbara Efrat, the Curator of Linguistics at the British Columbia Provincial Museum. Her immediate reaction was that one could compile a word list without necessarily understanding the language. I have not seen any sentences or longer passages in the Spanish records of the Indian languages and without these it is not possible to prove how well the Indians and their interlocutors understood each other.

Dr. Efrat could identify a number of the Spanish phonetic renderings with words in the Wakashan languages as they exist to-day, although the full range of sounds used by the Indians cannot be represented by the Roman alphabet. A linguist writing the Wakashan languages would need to use about forty-seven symbols or combinations of symbols in order to transcribe the languages adequately.

Some of Moziño's phonetic renderings are therefore difficult to identify with the Wakashan words for the given Spanish definitions. However, by and large, Dr. Efrat could identify the words given by Moziño with modern Wakashan. The Spanish meanings of these words are still applicable.

I was able to identify a few of the words because they have come into use in the lingua franca known to linguists as the Chinook Jargon which was still used on the Coast in my boyhood. *Klutsma* means a woman, *mo huec* or *moech* means a deer, and *clush* means good. *Tenas*, which to Moziño meant "little boy," can mean this in the Chinook lingua franca, although it often means just "little."

The extent of Moziño's vocabulary is indicated by his word list, which is given in the Appendix of this book, with an English translation. There are several variant lists in different manuscript copies of the *Noticias*; the one reproduced herein is from the version printed in Mexico in 1913. It includes most of the parts of speech. No conjugations for the verbs are given in the vocabulary itself, but an example using the verb *comer* (to eat) appears in Moziño's article on the Nootka language. While he could not master all the tenses and persons of this verb, he did cover most of those in common use, including negative and interrogative forms. These are reproduced in the Appendix.

The balance of probabilities is that the Indians and Spaniards understood each other well, an opinion I share with Vancouver and with several American traders. Nonetheless, in writing of what Moziño told us about the Indian system of government and about other subjects to follow, I am conscious of the possibility of error, and of the need to verify the accounts if possible.

87

Governmental power lay entirely in the hands of the chiefs, who held office by heredity and formed alliances by marriages with relatives of chiefs of other tribes, a system which would have seemed to Moziño to be just like Spain. The chief was an autocrat and it seemed to Moziño that he dealt with criminals quite arbitrarily, although there were some recognized crimes with recognized punishments. This may indicate that justice was less arbitrary than Moziño thought. While Moziño was at Nootka Maquinna sentenced a man to death for taking a nine-year-old girl into the forest and "using" her. He asked Quadra to send some food to the man's family afterwards since they would have nothing to eat with the breadwinner gone. Moziño had also noted that food was shared equally by all people, so it occurs to me that the withholding of food might be part of the punishment or deterrent as we call it.

The penalty for seducing a wife of the chief was death for the man and degradation to the status of *meschisme* for the woman. If the man was a prince the sentence was reduced to banishment. These transgressions may have been considered as crimes against property, of course. There was no problem with theft among the Indians since all inanimate property was communal with the chief acting as a trustee. If Captain John Kendrick were around he might snort and say that they would steal the ship if it wasn't anchored down. (I said *among* the Indians, Captain. You weren't the only visitor to complain about the habit some of the Indians had of taking anything off the ships that might be useful. Spaniards had backs like other men, and when they were turned...)

Although food was shared freely, the chief directed its storage and preservation and organized the seasonal migrations from place to place as required by the fish runs. When the tribe moved, the houses were dismantled and carried to the next site. Sometimes long planks were lashed across two or three canoes and loaded with house materials or personal effects. The journal of a Franciscan friar written in 1789 says that the house posts were left in place when the Indians moved. This implies that there were fixed village sites used seasonally from year to year.[15]

The organization of the food supply was the most important duty of the chief. Another duty was sacrifice, not to offer sacrifices, but to make them himself. He could only go to his wives at the full moon, and whenever there was a major famine he must forego that and retire to a rectangular box to lament, holding his body perfectly rigid for hours.

Moziño described another sacrifice. A chief would go to a freshwater lake nearby and take in hand the roughest pieces of bark he could find. He would then dive into the water and rub his face as hard as he could with the bark. He would continue until he had lost as much blood as he could stand, while the people admired him from the bank. Moziño could not find out the reason or the occasion for this ceremony.

There is one subject in Moziño's account I will mention only in passing. He thought that the Indian people were occasional cannibals, but other writers deny that there was any evidence of this. Other than this, at no place does any writer of the time whose works I have read mention the sacrifice of other people or of animals. Sacrifice was self-inflicted and was confined to the chiefs.

There were celebrations as well as sacrifices. While Moziño was at Nootka a daughter of Maquinna reached puberty. Her name had been Apenas and until that time she ran around freely with the other children and often came with her father to visit Quadra. At the onset of puberty her name was changed to the more dignified "Istocotli-tlemos" and a great celebration was held in her honour. A platform was set up, with a balcony above it, on which sat the new princess Istocotli-tlemos, formally dressed and wearing heavy copper jewelry. Maquinna and his brother then led her forward and introduced her by her new name.

The chiefs and nobility sang and danced and were given appropriate gifts. Then came the great wrestling match. Twenty or thirty men assembled on the ground, all having set aside their capes and hats, and Maquinna's brother threw a block of wood among them. There was a great struggle until finally one man gained possession of the block and was able to hang on. He was awarded a shell and another bout was started. The Spanish sailors stripped and joined the fray. When one of them won, the prize was a sea otter skin. Moziño and one of the Spanish chaplains also danced in honour of the princess, which greatly pleased her father.

This is Moziño's account of the celebration.

Quadra's journal also describes it, giving the new name of the Princess as Es-to-coti Tle-meg.[16] Es-to-coti or Istocotli appears in the word lists as "abalone shell," a much-prized decoration, but I have found no probable meaning for the rest of the Princess' name. Quadra describes the wrestling match for possession of the piece of wood and says that the participation of his sailors "appeared to take place in the most natural way." One of the chiefs, Quicomacia, put on *"un Bayle de Máscara."* This "masked ball" represented the movements of animals, and is one of the Coast Indians' traditions which has survived. Not to be outdone, Hupanamul entertained with naval manoeuvres in one of the largest canoes Quadra had seen. The paddlers executed three turns in the bay, rhythmically striking the sides of the canoe with their paddles, and singing a hymn in praise of friendship, without needing a *"Maestro de Capella."* One wonders how Quadra could know the subject matter of the hymn.

The celebrations lasted for several days, then Istocotli-tlemos was taken home and placed in front of a loom. She was told that now she was a woman and must set an example to the others by her industrious weaving. She was to be seen no more, since it would be risking disaster from the gods if she left the house for the next ten months. She seems to have been a great favourite of Quadra, and he asked many times if she could come with her father when he visited, as she had done before. This was refused with apparently genuine regret, but Maquinna did finally relent to the extent of letting her wave good-bye from a distance once or twice after Quadra had visited him.

The spiritual life of the Indians, said Moziño, centred on a Creator and a Destroyer. In the beginning a woman lived alone in the forest, which was populated by deer without horns and dogs without tails. Geese without wings swam on the water in front of her home. She was so lonely that she wept day and night. The Creator took pity on her and sent to her a canoe made of shining copper paddled by fine young men with strong round arms. One of the men told her that the Creator had seen her loneliness and would give her a companion. She cried all the more and blew her nose into the sand. Looking down, she found that one of the drops had turned into a tiny man. At the same time, antlers grew on the heads of the deer, the dogs started wagging their new tails, and she heard the clap of wings as the birds took off from the water.

She was told to pick up the squirming little man and put him in a small shell. As he grew, she was to transfer him to larger and larger shells. She did this, and before too long he grew to full size and gave her proof of his manhood. She then bore a son who became the first chief. Other sons became the first *meschismes*. Meschismes were commoners or slaves, according to the point of view of the European observer.

Moziño does not ascribe any anthropomorphic characteristics to the Creator, but the Destroyer lives in the mountains and is monstrous and hairy. I wonder if that might be why the men went beardless, plucking out the hairs with shell tweezers? The Destroyer had a human head, a bear's fangs, and an eagle's claws. He could knock down a man with a shout and his slap would break one into a thousand pieces.

After death the souls of chiefs and princes ascend to Glory and are united with the Creator, while the souls of meschismes go to Hell. Caamaño's version is a bit different from Moziño's. He just says the place of the dead chiefs is above the earth and that of the meschismes is below, without ascribing any glorious or hellish attributes to these domains. For this reason the bodies of chiefs are hung in trees and those of meschismes are buried in the earth, to be close to their appointed places in the hereafter. Quadra's own journal agrees with Caamaño in this respect.[17] He says that although the meschismes go to "*el Infierno*" they do not suffer the pains which torment men of understanding. Other than this, Quadra's version is an abbreviation of Moziño's, with minor differences.

There are some difficulties with this part of Moziño's account. As careful an observer as he was, even Moziño could hardly have stepped into the Indian spirit in a stay of only five months. His description of the hereditary rulership is similar to European practice, and his description of heaven and hell reflects the mystique of the Christian religion. There are differences, of course. The attainment of heaven, like the attainment of chieftaincy, is an accident of birth.

There is less difficulty in accepting the authenticity of his account of the Creation legend itself. It does not reflect the Christian religion. In fact, the role of the woman is more like that of the father than that of the mother of the first chief. The Creation legend still exists and is known to the Indian people as far south as the Makah Nation near Cape Flattery and as far north as Kyuquot, which is near the northern end of Vancouver Island. The Makah Cultural Centre has a sculpture of the tiny man in a mussel shell. This is one of the objects recovered at Ozette.

The Ozette houses had already been buried under the mud for three centuries when Moziño visited Nootka. One must not overdraw the parallels between the Ozette artifacts and the Mexican's account, nor is the best scientific advice a substitute for direct experience. I decided to seek another opinion, that of the Indians themselves. I set off for the **place mistakenly called Nootka.**

The people have corrected Captain Cook's mistake and again call themselves the Mowachaht: the people of the deer. Most of them live at Gold River now, and that is where I found the Hereditary Chief, Ambrose Maquinna.

"It's the blue and white house," says Margarita James, the Band Manager, pointing past the TV satellite dish. The ground is not muddy, but when I go inside I take off my shoes as requested by the sign pinned on the door. The chief is sitting in his armchair inside, with three grandchildren playing opposite him. Their interest in the stranger lasts only for a few moments. They resume their play while we talk, joined occasionally by their mother who has other things to do.

After a few minutes I start on the Spanish vocabulary of the language of the Mowachaht. First I try *tagetchite*. I have to go through some of the variants: *tag-hite*, *tag-cite* and .... "Oh," says the Chief, "you mean the head," and he gives me the correct pronunciation. I feel what I can only describe as a rushing sensation within me as the door to the eighteenth century begins to open.

91

I try *caa-hsi*. He takes a moment to think and says it must be *casi*, which means eye. Another good fit. *Nitsa* for "nose" is recognized instantly.

As we go through some of the words the door to the eighteenth century opens wider. Word after word he agrees with the Spanish interpretation of his language. There is some difficulty with verbs. The Spanish didn't understand the tenses and persons of verbs. *Texpitl* or something like it means "being seated." The Chief says that if you ask someone to sit down there is a longer form, which he gives me. My apology for sitting down before I was asked is waved aside. As we progress there is only one complete miss. *Gua-gua-mi-tic* does not mean a fishing net — or anything else the Chief could think of. A net is *tsima*. (Ingraham and Martinez knew this in 1789.) Chief Maquinna doesn't agree with the word for "chief." The nearest he could come to the Spanish *tais* is *tyee* which means an older brother.

A chief is *ya(h)wich*, with the "ch" sounding like the Scottish "loch."

Coa-utch or *coa-uts* is not "grandfather." He points to a small boy (who gives us a quick smile) and says "He is my *coa-uts*, I am his *na-ec-so*," which Moziño gives as "grandson." Apparently the meanings were reversed at some stage in the transcription. The *Relación* of Galiano's voyage published in 1802 partly corrected this. It gave *coa-utch* for both grandfather and grandson.

We two na-ec-sos come to the words for "wind." *Oco-maha* means good weather rather than a fair wind. There is no one word for wind, the Chief says, because each wind brings different weather or blows at different times. A westerly is a *huchslekl*, an easterly is called *tukchi* and the winter wind from the north is *yuk-yukw*. He is interested to hear that in a similar way the Inuit have no one word for snow, because it takes many forms, each with its own uses and dangers.

The conversation changes from words to the stories in Quadra's and Moziño's accounts. I start to describe the wrestling match which took place at the inauguration of the new princess, in which a block of wood is thrown into the crowd of young men. Chief Maquinna interjects, "It was usually about the size of a rugby ball." He tells me that another way of playing the game was to throw in a bundle of sticks about the size of Chinese chopsticks. One of the sticks was marked, and it was the winner. He recognizes the description of Hupanamul and his men paddling their great canoe around the harbour as a salute, singing and rapping the canoe with their paddles. This is just the way it was done.

Chief Maquinna has never heard of a chief jumping into the water and scrubbing his face with bark. Hemlock branches, not bark, and not until it drew blood. He shows me how a bundle of hemlock branches can be twisted in the hands and rubbed on the body. It is like soap, and it's very healthy. He used to do it himself. Before hunting whales, or even seals, a hunter would rub himself all over with hemlock branches. This sometimes went on for several days without the hunter even going home, so he would be absolutely clean. In the Chief's own lifetime this was done before hunting for deer, because after the body was cleaned in this way the deer could not smell the hunter.

* * *

I put on my shoes (for which the Mowachan word is "shoes," says the Hereditary Chief with a smile) and step outside into the twentieth century.

The next day I am introduced to Rene de Waal who works in the Gold River pulp mill. He has agreed to take me in his boat to Santa Cruz de Nutca (Friendly Cove). Norman Paulson, who has spent eighteen years in the area and knows everyone, comes along to make the introductions. When we reach Nootka Sound we motor out to sea for a mile or so and approach the cove from the west as Galiano did, keeping a good bit more than a musket shot from the rocks at the entrance of the cove. There is a lighthouse where the fort used to be, but the beach looks the same as it does in Cardero's drawing, including the spot where Meares had his building and launched the first ship built in the Pacific Northwest.

Ray Williams comes to meet us and takes us home for a cup of coffee. He and his wife Terry are both members of the Mowachaht Band. They have lived all their lives at Yuquot, which was the name of the village before Captain Cook innocently re-christened it. For the last fifteen years the Williams family have been the only residents. Their children are in high school now, two sons living with friends in Victoria and a daughter in Nanaimo. Both Ray's father and Terry's father died last year in their nineties, and since then their only neighbour has been their friend Ed, who has been the lightkeeper for years.

I tell Ray and Terry about my visit with the Hereditary Chief, and go through a few of the words. Terry puts down the beaded necklace she is making and listens to my pronunciation (with some amusement, I think) but she agrees that the Spanish got the words right. The wrestling match with the block of wood is called *tupati*. It was played in the same way a century and a half after the Spanish left.

"There are songs about the Spaniards and their time at Yuquot," Ray tells me "All the songs of my people are happy songs. If there was something sad we did not sing about it, except for a song about someone who has died. We are sad when someone dies whom we have loved, but we are happy that they lived, so that is really not a sad song. The songs which my father sang are about the good relationships with the Spaniards. If they had been bad people there would be no songs."

Ray's father had seen the old Spanish well, but it's all filled in and gone now. It had a brick lining and the bricks were rounded at the corners, not like our bricks.

We walk along past the place where the Spanish buildings used to be. There is one totem pole, carved about 1920. It is starting to deteriorate, and has a noticeable lean towards the north. Totem poles have their life span, just as people do, and when it is over they die and rot. Personally I do not regard this as the loss of a work of art, but as a natural process which it is perhaps unwise to interrupt by embalming the pole. I'm not sure Ray or Terry would agree with me and I know that museum people would not, but I prefer to see the art of the totem pole continue to grow and change naturally, as it has done ever since the white men brought iron tools.

We retrace our steps and then walk along a path by the ocean beach to the lake where Maquinna bathed. Ray's kids swim in the sea when they are home in the summer, then jump into the lake, which is warmer. They don't use hemlock branches or bark but Ray says Maquinna did use bark and he rubbed himself all over, drawing blood. He would be at the lake several days eating nothing. He would go all the way around the lake, scrubbing himself and jumping in the water. His wife would be the only person with him and she was there just in case he passed out after jumping in the water. It was like praying, and the reason was that Maquinna wanted a safe and successful whale hunt or seal hunt. The name of the ceremony was *usumchl*.

On the way back to the house Ray cuts some *kechlsoop* shoots. He tries to teach me the "chl" sound, made by putting the tongue behind the upper front teeth and letting air out of the corners of the mouth, but my "chl" doesn't sound like his "chl." If the Spaniards had the same difficulty it didn't prevent them from writing the words in a way the Williamses can recognize.

Back at the house Ray peels the kechlsoop and we sit around the table and eat it, dipping the shoots in the sugar bowl to reduce the spicy taste. The Latin name for kechlsoop is *Heracleum lanatum,* and in English it's called cow parsnip. No, I'm not a botanist, but when I got home I looked it up.[18] The four of us, Ray, Terry, my friend Norm, and myself, finish the kechlsoop before we leave.

***

I have an invitation to go along on a helicopter trip to Kyuquot on the following day, which I am delighted to accept. Kyuquot is upcoast from Nootka Island, but the language and customs of the Kyuquots are similar to those of the Mowachaht, and I have been told that the former chief of the Kyuquots knows a lot about the history of his people.

Verna Hansen comes down to meet the "chopper." She is active in village affairs and has offered to take me along to meet the chief.

His name is Willie Harry, but soon I am Jack and he is Willie. He uses a wheel chair now and a cold has left him short of breath, but you can see that he has been an active man, and he knows some of the people I knew on the coast years ago. I trot out my word lists, and he recognizes the words. We don't spend much time on this but go on to some of the stories. The wrestling game is called *pacheksma-achl* in Kyuquot. *"Pachek"* means a gift or prize, and he thinks that may be the origin of the word "potlatch." I think his "chl" may be a bit different to the way Terry Williams would pronounce it.

He says that the song sung by Hupanamul's paddlers would give the names of the visitors and the reasons for the visit, and no one would land until they had announced themselves in this way and been invited. I think for a moment of Pedro Santa Ana.

Now I start to tell the legend of the first man, to see whether the Spanish got it right. Indian people do not today have large houses. There are one or two other adults in the room as well as a baby and some small children. As I speak the room quietens down. When I am finished Willie says one word,*"Antoak."* I ask him what that means. It's the name of the boy in the mussel shell.

The room is completely quiet now and I notice a few more people have slipped in, including a lad who might be fourteen or so. He listens to every word as Willie carries the story further. The Kyuquots say that when Antoak grew up he had two sons. One settled at Kyuquot and the other at a place near where Port Hardy is now. The brother from Port Hardy came to Kyuquot. There is a swampy lake nearby with a little creek leading into the sea. The brother told the Kyuquot chief that he could bring sockeye salmon into the lake but the chief said, "No, sockeye only come for one month but we must eat all year. We have fish with hands which are always here."

Antoak could see a beam in the sky which no one else could see. Bows and arrows were used in those days, so one day Antoak shot an arrow in the sky and it stuck in the beam. Then he shot another arrow and the point of that one stuck in the end of the first. He shot more arrows and each one stuck in the end of the last one. So it was like a rope and he climbed the rope up into the skies and was gone.

I climb into the helicopter and soon I too am gone.

* * *

On the flight back to Gold River, on the drive down Vancouver Island, on the ferry trip home, I wondered what I could write. I am not qualified to argue with the scholars or to express an expert opinion on what the Indians have told me. I decided I could say this, and I think it is important to do so: this is how it appeared to the Spaniards, this is what they told us, and to this extent it is supported by the findings at Ozette, by the words of the modern Indian language, and by the legends and ceremonies as they are remembered today by the Indian people.

Interlude

THE FUR TRADE

The account of Captain James Cook's third voyage was published in 1784. It included the story of the sale of sea otter pelts in Canton at high prices, high enough to suggest large profits. On August 9, 1785 a vessel which had been re-named *Sea Otter* arrived at Nootka from Macao under the command of James Hanna.[1] The first word spoken by the Indians was *Makook,* a word recorded in the Nootka vocabulary compiled by James Cook[2] and later to appear in the Quadra-Moziño vocabulary as *ma-cu-co.*[3] It meant trade. At the time of Hanna's arrival the Indians at Nootka had seen at most three sailing ships: Perez's *Santiago* in 1774 and Cook's *Resolution* and *Discovery* in 1778. It is a mistake to think that Hanna and other English and American sea-captains seeking furs introduced the Indian people to trade. If Hanna or the others who followed him had any such ideas they would soon have found out they were wrong. Beads and baubles were accepted as gifts by the Indians and salmon was offered as a response or simply as a gesture to the newcomers. This was not trade, any more than buying a customer a good lunch and letting him pay for the drinks is trade. It was a preliminary move to establish a friendly relationship.

For real trade, iron was in great demand, as were other metals such as copper. Iron was most acceptable in thin strips, which could easily be made into knives and harpoon points similar to implements already in use.[4] It had to be malleable and free from flaws so that it could be fabricated by cold working. Once the demand for metal was satisfied the fur traders had to switch to other goods. In 1788-9 Kendrick had his blacksmith working all winter making iron chisels for trade.[5] By 1795 when John Boit visited the coast, he could not give "chizz'ls" away as presents although he found a ready acceptance of blankets and cloth.[6] Muskets were popular trade items for a time, then the demand shifted to powder and shot.

It would be another mistake to think that the Europeans bought furs from Indian hunters. On the contrary, all trade at Nootka was conducted through Maquinna, and at other places it was the chief who traded. There is some evidence that Maquinna acted as a wholesaler, procuring furs from other tribes by trade — or raid.[7] Galiano's people discovered in 1792 that a sea otter pelt at Nootka was worth one sheet of copper, whereas three similar skins on the other side of Vancouver Island could be purchased from the Nimpkish for two sheets of copper.[8] The 1792 price, incidentally, was ten times the price paid by the first traders. It is yet another mistake to think that a market works only when there is a large number of buyers and sellers.

Another dimension of the market appeared when the chiefs began to get rich. The demand shifted from useful articles to sheets of copper, the mass of a sheet being standardized at one-half arroba or approximately five kilograms. The traders wondered what the chiefs did with all this copper. While a small amount could be used for decorative articles, iron or brass was much better for making tools or weapons. The answer was that the chiefs did nothing with the copper. They just owned it.

This seems to have puzzled the Europeans, but Moziño found the answer.[9] Although it could be used as a medium of exchange, its main function was to serve as a symbol of wealth, or as the economists would put it, a repository of value. In Spain gold served the same purpose.

In the sixteenth century, Spain overran Central America and the northern part of South America. The objective was gold, which in some places was used profusely for ornamentation by the aboriginal people. Throughout Europe gold became very cheap. All the conquistador had to do was to knock the native on the head and take his gold collar. As a result the owners of gold could pay high prices and still live well while those who had no gold could not afford the means of sustenance.

At Nootka there is slight evidence of a similar inflation. Wealth from the fur trade did not trickle down to the hunters of sea otter.[10] It took a lot of time to hunt for these animals, prepare the pelts and transport them to Maquinna's house, and make trade journeys to other tribes to procure more. This time could not be spent catching and drying fish or moving the village from place to place to follow seasonal fluctuations in food sources. As a result, in spite of the improvement in fishing and hunting equipment Malaspina found the Indians short of food.[11] The narrator of Galiano's voyage made a similar remark. Eliza had shared his meagre supplies with the Indians at one point.[12]

The Indians were not conquered, and no effective sovereignty of a European or American power was established during the years of the maritime fur trade. I suggest that the Indian system of government and the organization of their society were not deeply disturbed, nor did methods of fishing and hunting change radically. They had iron fishhooks and, for a time, stronger fishing lines. Muskets had about the same range as an arrow but the noise and the time required to reload would have been a drawback in hunting. Their demand for iron tools was for ones similar in form to their tools of bone, antler, shell, or stone.[13]

When the fur trade dwindled the Indians were left for another generation much as they had been, but with better tools and equipment, muskets without powder or shot, and venereal disease. We do not know whether this was introduced or had been there all along. The depletion of the sea otter population did not matter in the least. By that time, copper or blankets had replaced fur as the symbol of wealth.

THE STRAIT OF JUAN DE FUCA

Galiano was not able to refit his ships at Nootka as he would have wished, but he did get new masts for *Mexicana* and he was able to replace some of the running rigging which was constantly breaking because of poor quality.

From a drawing of the two ships it appears that *Mexicana* was restored to her original mixed brigantine/schooner rig, without upper (i.e. topgallant) sails. Eliza was living ashore, as he had done since 1790, and his frigate *Concepción* was rigged down. Galiano was given *Concepción's* launch, which he cut down to a length that could be accommodated aboard his small ships, and he repaired *Sutil's* boat, which may have been damaged in the *Mexicana* dismasting incident. Four additional crewmen were picked up, including a carpenter and a caulker. *Aranzazu* arrived during their stay, and the leech from this vessel volunteered to join them. Galiano was assured of the leech's skill in the practice of medicine, so he took this Luis Galvez into *Sutil* and passed on to his junior officer Valdés the jailbound leech whom they had picked up in Acapulco. Galvez has the distinction of being the only member of the crew of *Sutil* and *Mexicana* to be mentioned by name.

The relationship between Quadra and Galiano was uneasy. Quadra's naval rank of *capitan de navio* was senior to Galiano's, but if Galiano's instructions were the same as Maurelle's, whom he replaced, he would have been operating under the direct orders of the Viceroy, responsible only to him. Also, whereas Maurelle was one of Quadra's officers, Galiano was a *peninsular* nominated by Malaspina. A peninsular was a person resident in Spain. In the eyes of a creole he was one step below a *gachupin* who, although born in Spain, at least had the good sense to live in the Americas. The peninsular would of course have exactly the opposite view.

Naturally, Galiano wanted his ships in top condition for the Juan de Fuca voyage but facilities at Nootka were limited and the weather was wretched. Galiano wrote a rather patronizing letter to Quadra saying

Circumnavigation of Vancouver Island.

(Arran Rapids)
Angostura de los Comandantes

Brazo de la Tabla
(Toba Inlet)

Brazo de Vernaci
(Knight Inlet)

(Point Grey)
Punta de Langara

(Point Roberts)
Punta de Cepeda

Isla de
San Juan

Córdoba
(Esquimalt)

Cala del Descanso
(Descanso Bay)

Nuñez Gaona
(Neah Bay)

Gold River

Nutka
(Yuquot)

Kyuquot

Cabo Scot
(Cape Scott)

50° North

48° North

that he greatly appreciated the assistance afforded by the latter which was sufficient to enable his ships to do their job, but he asked Quadra to report the details of this assistance to the Viceroy, and also to inform His Excellency that *Sutil* and *Mexicana* sailed from Nootka with some shortages, namely a pit saw, sail cloth, and tallow. Quadra sent him on his way with an order on Fidalgo, who was within the Strait (of Juan de Fuca) and sent copies of all the correspondence to the Viceroy.[1] It seems to me that Galiano was much too arrogant in his dealings with Quadra, a senior officer who had been on the northern coast battling weather, disease, and Indians in a ship smaller than *Sutil* when Galiano was a fifteen-year-old apprentice officer.

On June 2, three weeks after their arrival, the goletas left Nootka at four o'clock in the morning on the land breeze in order to clear the point called Arrecifes to the southwest. This time the newly acquired launch went ahead and they managed to stay off the ground. The early start was made because the land breeze regularly died between ten a.m. and noon as the westerly began to fill in. They took the launch aboard, made sail, and off they went; only the easterly land breeze veered to the south and stayed there. So on went the goletas, and as sailors say, "tacked on the header," turning to the southeast and relying on the tide to carry them round the point clear of its outlying reefs which lay dead ahead. It didn't work, so they turned back to Nootka and groped their way back to port in rain, fog, and a rising southeaster. Galiano did then what in my view he should have done in the first place. He consulted Maquinna, whose men lived by fishing from canoes and survived by being sufficiently weather-wise to keep out of trouble. Maquinna, who must have had a good sense of timing, said more or less, "Leave it to me," and started intoning prayers for a *"clus nas"* or good sky, with appropriate facial contortions. Even then the Spaniards nearly jeopardized their chances by laughing at Maquinna, but were restrained by his young men. On the fourth of June, Maquinna told them the weather was settled. The voyagers went to his house to thank him and were offered a treat of whale meat. It seems to have been pretty rank stuff, but Maquinna was satisfied when Valdés (at Galiano's orders?) tasted it. The Spaniards did not want to refuse the whale meat and thereby compound the errors they had made by laughing at Maquinna's prayers.

The next morning *Sutil* and *Mexicana* left. This time they were towed out at 2:30 a.m. and had the boats aboard half an hour later. With a good northwest wind Galiano decided to lay his course directly for Arrecifes Point. He made it, but it seems that Maquinna arranged to leave them becalmed later in the morning so they would understand the dangers of unseemly laughter. However, in a couple of hours the westerly began to blow and the goletas ran before it all day, logging seven knots, the best speed in all the voyage. The day gave way to a clear moonlit night, which meant that the officers could relax. Before daylight the wind dropped and when the sun came up the entrance to the Strait of Juan de Fuca was in sight and the goletas were drifting nicely in with the tide. *"Un pedazo de pasteleria"* said the helmsman to his relief, or whatever slang was used in those days meaning "It's a piece of cake." I don't have authorities for the last sentence but when you run into the Strait on a moonlit night in June with a following tide and the westerly dies as the sun rises over the distant mountains what else can you say?

As the morning passed, kelp could be seen along the Vancouver Island shore and although there was no wind and not a very strong current the ships drifted into choppy water. The chop and the kelp were known to be signs of shallow water but the leadsman reported a depth of thirty-two fathoms, probably on the edge of Soquel Bank. At eleven o'clock the westerly began. Some Nitinat Indians were out fishing and gave *Mexicana* a large fish in exchange for a knife.

The goletas crossed over to the south side and made for Nuñez Gaona, known to us as Neah Bay. Fidalgo was at Nuñez Gaona, in the much-travelled frigate *Princesa*. He had been there a month, says the narrator, although "a week" would have been more accurate since it was then June 6 and he had arrived May 28.[2] Fidalgo had come at Quadra's orders, prepared to establish a settlement if it was so decided. He had brought the necessary tools and equipment, but not the twenty-five to thirty married men referred to in the Viceroy's instructions. He had already planted a garden and built a shed and a stockade for livestock in which four cannons were later installed.[3] In the event, as we shall see, the settlement was never built, and it was to be many years before a second European establishment was to be attempted in what is now the State of Washington.

The natives were friendly, and there was a small boy who offered to bring women out to *Sutil* and *Mexicana*. The Spaniards inferred that these women were slaves, as were the boys offered in the same way at Nootka. The Spanish reply to this offer is not recorded but the narrator did say that the women of Nuñez Gaona were not embarrassed in their canoes or on shore by their lack of underclothing and two of them, who had well proportioned features, were so fair of skin that they could be called white.

After charting the harbour at Nuñez Gaona, including an island in the middle of the bay, *Sutil* and *Mexicana* left, relieving the waiting Fidalgo of a pit saw, some tallow, and medicines which Quadra had been unable to supply. There is no mention of the sail cloth.

103

Mexicana had taken a passenger aboard at Nuñez Gaona. He was a visiting chief named Tetacus who wanted to be dropped off at his own village at Córdoba (on Vancouver Island). His wives, like other sailors' wives since, wanted no part of this sailboat business. They preferred to travel by canoe. In fact they tried hard to talk Tetacus out of going with the Spaniards. A canoe might be a bit slower but it seemed a lot safer, as familiar craft often do.

They made sail and were underway just after noon. Does one follow the American shore or the Canadian shore? This question is debated annually in about fifty yachts in the Swiftsure race. The debate aboard the goletas was similar. Someone pointed out that although the breeze in the harbour was from the southeast the weather was fair and this undoubtedly meant that there would be a westerly along the American shore. At that time it was just the southern shore; the United States were thousands of miles away, on the other side of the Mississippi River.

It is always advisable to plan ahead if you want to win a yacht race or find the Northwest Passage. The southern shore was chosen and the two commanders made their way out of the harbour. They found there was a flat calm as far as one could see along the southern shore, including the place where the ships were. Some ripples caused by a breeze could be seen offshore, so a boat was launched to tow out and reach the breeze.

Tetacus helped the wind along with a silent invocation, stretching out his arm, doubling first one then all his fingers, opening two of them, raising one and leaving it for a while. Presumably these gestures were acceptable to the wind gods or else the Spaniards were wrong about the invocation and Tetacus' gestures were intended to express his opinion of the people who had wanted to follow the southern side of the Strait.

Only one boat towing one ship is mentioned. Perhaps *Sutil* had picked up a puff. The other *bicho* always seems to do this.

On reaching the breeze they sailed off towards the *northern* shore and coasted along on a fair northwester, which lasted out the day and continued all night. It was another clear night, and any ruffled feelings over the choice of the wrong course would have been soothed by the sound of the water frothing along the bow and by the faint hiss of the wake, which would turn up bubbles of phosphorescence trailing behind and below the ship like stars; pure light, *sin calor y sin color*, without heat or colour. Unfortunately the narrator omitted to say this, so I have had to rely on my own experience as a guide.

At daylight they came to the Punta Morena de la Vega and Tetacus advised them to pass inside the outlying rocks. Any experienced sailor today would advise his skipper to go inside Race Rocks on a westerly, and evidently Tetacus knew his Strait. He advised his hosts to stop and take in fresh water which was scarce farther along the coast, but there was a good supply aboard so they pressed on.

Tetacus seems to have been quite at home aboard ship. He slept and ate well and took a keen interest in seamanship and navigation. His hosts credited him with the ability to recognize points on Eliza's map, and he knew the names of all the English and Spanish captains who had called at Nuñez Gaona or sailed in the Strait.[4] Among the former were "Wancower and Broton." This was the first intimation of Vancouver's presence. All this suggests that although Tetacus is the first recorded hitch-hiker in the Pacific Northwest it may not have been his first voyage.

Later in the morning three canoes approached *Mexicana* but their occupants were unwilling to moor alongside. The Indians were wearing woollen blankets and had some new ones in the canoes which they offered in exchange for a sheet of copper. Tetacus was a grateful guest and gave Vernaci four beautifully-crafted copper bracelets he was wearing, to trade for the blankets. Vernaci tried out the vendors by offering to trade two of the bracelets for one blanket, but Tetacus said he should give all four. Vernaci was unwilling to accept this sacrifice on the part of Tetacus and declined to trade. In the end the Indians gave Valdés some black fig-like fruit with a floury texture and a taste of saltpeter and they parted friends.

The blankets offered for sale by the Indians were evidently woven and probably made of dog hair. Mountain goat hair or spun sea otter fur are less likely materials at Córdoba and sheep were unknown. The identity of the fruit is questionable; it has been suggested the Indians gave Vernaci dried clams.[5]

The goletas anchored in Córdoba harbour at eleven in the morning. The wives of Tetacus were not there to see the finish, but their canoes arrived two hours later, just as Tetacus began to show signs of anxiety. An unremarkable twenty-four-hour passage for the ships, but an impressive canoe voyage in my view.

Interlude

EIGHTEENTH-CENTURY NAVIGATION

Galiano had not yet done any exploring. He was following the 1791 map, which was based on the explorations of Quimper, Pantoja and Narvaez; the latter two under Eliza's command. To make or to use such a map, obviously one had to know where one was on the face of the earth. How did the Spanish navigators do this, and how good were their calculations of latitude and longitude?

Latitude is easy to estimate. It is the altitude of the north (or south) pole above the horizon. Christopher Columbus used Stella Maris, the Star of the Sea (which we call the Pole Star), to navigate across the Atlantic and, more importantly, to find his way back to Spain. Apart from two minor difficulties he did not have much trouble. The first was that he had only crude instruments for measuring the altitude of Stella Maris above the horizon. The second was that he only discovered when he was part of the way across that Stella Maris is not exactly at the north pole. This he found out by measuring the magnetic variation each morning and night. It appeared to change back and forth, and he guessed correctly that it was because the star goes around the pole in a small circle. His measurement of its direction natually changed with it.

By the end of the eighteenth century science had progressed. By then, it was known how far north or south of the equator the sun was on any particular day, and how far north or south the major fixed stars were, including Stella Maris. Also, sextants had been developed which were quite accurate. At sea, latitude could be determined by a noon sight of the sun, probably within a mile or so. Ashore, one could do even better. An artificial horizon was used, which was a dish containing a pool of mercury. One measured the angle between the sun and its reflection off the surface of the mercury, then divided it by two. Using this method, the latitude of the Spanish observatory at Nootka was measured to within twenty seconds, or a third of a sea mile of its value as shown on modern maps.

Longitude is quite another matter. We are aware that when it is noon in Halifax it is eight in the morning in Victoria. There was no standard time in Galiano's day. In fact its invention is attributed to Sanford Fleming, the first chief engineer of the Canadian Pacific Railway who read a paper entitled "The Adoption of a Prime Meridian" to an International Geographical Congress in 1880.[1] In Galiano's time, and for ninety years after his exploration of the Pacific Northwest, longitude was simply the difference between the sun time where you were, and the sun time at some other place. Galiano used Acapulco as his point of reference, because it was his port of departure. His maps were corrected to give longitude west of Cadiz. Other Spanish maps show longitude *west* of Tenerife, while the English maps show longitude *east* of Greenwich.

Galiano could measure local sun time by observations of the sun or stars; the problem was to know what time it was in Acapulco at the same instant. If he had had an accurate clock he could have set it before he left Acapulco and then not touched it, except for winding it. Unfortunately the clock, or chronometer, just could not be sufficiently accurate, especially as it had to stand up to the rigours of a long sea voyage in an unheated wooden ship. Today you can buy a quartz watch for about twenty-five dollars which will do a much better job than anything that was available in the eighteenth century, and you can check it by a radio signal which is accurate to some ridiculously small fraction of a second.

Galiano's ships each had a chronometer and what he called a pocket clock. The latter would have been some sort of timepiece which could be carried about the ship, since the chronometer had to remain in its case, undisturbed except for winding. The pocket clock, or deck watch as I would call it, could be used to time an observation of the altitude of the sun or a star, then compared to the chronometer. This is the method I used in the 1960's with the help of some radio time signals.

The observation must be timed to the nearest second or two if the longitude is to be measured with the same accuracy as the latitude. This has to be done on a heaving deck. A star sight has to be taken in the brief minutes at dawn or dusk when both star and horizon can be seen. If it is cloudy, the navigator will have to hope it clears that night or the next morning. If the seas are large, be careful. Not only does one need a third hand to hang on, but he may find a star going up and down. This is not an undiscovered astronomical phenomenon like Columbus's Stella Maris; it means that what he thinks is the horizon is a series of passing waves, each five times the height of the deck above sea level.

It is not surprising that many eighteenth or nineteenth century ships would try to get into the latitude of their destination then run down their eastings (or westings) until they picked up their landfall. This works well enough if you are aiming at a continent and know which ocean you are in. If it is a small island you are after, it could be a long voyage if you do not know whether you are to the east or west of it.

These methods work fairly well if you are just bumbling about the ocean until you get somewhere, but Galiano was a hydrographer; his job was to map the coast and he had to fix positions with some degree of accuracy. He needed an accurate measure of time to calculate the error in his chronometers. He compared notes with other ships when he could and admired Vancouver's Arnold and Kendal chronometers. One of these is Arnold 176, now in the possession of the Maritime Museum in Vancouver. His own chronometer was Arnold 344.[2] Such a comparison gives some confidence to the navigators if both agree, but if they do not it leaves open the question of which is wrong.

Galiano is credited by his biographer with being the originator of a method of determining latitude by an observation of a star (probably Stella Maris) when it was not on the meridian.[3] He also knew how to measure Acapulco time by two methods.

The first method was lunar distances. We all know that the moon does not rise at the same time every night. Its position in relation to the sun or to the stars is changing steadily. At any instant the angle between the moon and the sun or stars is the same (or nearly so), regardless of one's position on earth. Salamanca or Vernaci could measure the angle between the moon and a chosen star (or occasionally the sun) and by means of tables prepared by the Royal Observatories in Spain, could calculate the time at Acapulco or Cadiz. This lunar distance changes very slowly, which means that it must be measured with great precision. Sometimes a hundred or more lunar distances would be measured in as close a time as possible, and the results averaged. Even so, I am surprised that such an observation was made only three weeks out from Acapulco and that the navigators had sufficient confidence in the series to feel that it confirmed the accuracy of the chronometer to within a quarter of a degree of longitude.

The second method was to observe the emergence or occasionally the eclipse, of one of the four major moons of Jupiter. The times of these emergences, expressed in sun time at Cadiz, or Paris or Greenwich for that matter, can be predicted and they are the same no matter where you happen to be. Tables for the moons of Jupiter had been developed as far back as Galileo's time, the early 17th century, and not much later there were mechanical models which, with the aid of tables, could be used to predict emergence times. Sometimes the tables were engraved on the instrument itself. Such an instrument is in the collection at the Museum of the History of Science in Firenza.[4] By 1792 astronomers had developed detailed predictions and, among other astronomical data, Galiano had sets of tables giving emergence times for Jupiter's satellites.

An observation of an emergence could only be made on shore. An astronomical telescope mounted on a fixed base was required, and such an insrument is included in the *estado* or manifest of both of Galiano's ships.[5] One of these was set up at Nootka on May 16 to observe the emergence of Jupiter's first satellite, but all that could be seen was clouds. A second attempt was made two days later but at that time Jupiter was not far behind the sun which had just set and in the half light the result was doubtful. It is not an easy observation. The observer's eye must be glued to the telescope at the instant the satellite pops into view, or he has missed it for that day.

There was another opportunity on the 25th, but it was raining. Finally on the 28th they got the second satellite of Jupiter and were able to fix the longitude at 120° 49' west of Cadiz. This was 19 minutes more than the doubtful observation of the 18th, 26 minutes more than the estimate made the year before by the even more doubtful method of lunar distances, and ironically it is 29 minutes, or about eighteen sea miles more than the longitude measured on a modern map. The problem was not in the field measurements but in the tables used by Galiano, which contained errors not discovered until later, including one of 29'45" for the emergence of May 28.[6] If our explorers had possessed correct tables they would have been out by one and a half minutes of longitude; less than a sea mile. This is a remarkable feat. It is not a remarkable coincidence because other observations when corrected for errors in the tables show almost the same accuracy.

At sea it is impossible to observe the satellites of Jupiter. With only a chronometer and an occasional opportunity for measuring lunar distances longitude was always uncertain. It is easy to understand why mariners thought the perils of the sea were much less than the perils of the shore.

11

THE GULF OF GEORGIA

E*l puerto de Córdoba es hermoso"* said the narrator. Wild roses were more plentiful at Córdoba than at Nootka, there were a lot of waterfowl about, and *Sutil* and *Mexicana* were comfortably anchored in their "six fathoms sand." All these things lent beauty to the harbour of Córdoba in the eyes of the explorers. Tetacus invited the officers ashore in the afternoon. There were only about fifty Indians in the village but the visitors were told that Tetacus was a great chief and it was evident that he commanded considerable respect and obedience. Cloaks were spread on the ground for the visitors to sit on and an octopus dinner was served. They were shown all possible courtesy, and the host embraced them when they returned, much satisfied, to the ships.

There was complete quiet at night. Since this is the normal situation at night in any uncrowded anchorage, it may be that the narrator commented on it because the party ashore had been rather noisy.

The flood started to run at three o'clock in the morning, so they left in order to take advantage of it, and of a light southerly breeze which filled in nicely as the sun got higher. The next night was spent at anchor off the southern tip of San Juan Island, a name which has survived but is now used in the plural. Indeed, the 1791 map shows it as the "Isla" and "Archipielago de San Juan." Galiano had no interest in the channels opening to the south, none of which seemed to run in the direction of the Atlantic Ocean. "We left these," said the narrator, "as being of minor importance and more appropriate for exploration in case we had to turn back, which we thought probable."

It is evident that Galiano did not expect to sail through the Northwest Passage to the Atlantic (in fact the ships were not provisioned for such a voyage) and he had not yet formed an intention of circumnavigating a possible Vancouver Island. Whether he knew or suspected it was an island is not clear. Later in the text no surprise is expressed when he finds the tide rising and falling with no perceptible current. I would infer that Galiano suspected our Vancouver Island was indeed an island but either did not expect to be able to get through to the north, or thought that having completed his mission it would be easier to return by the way he had come.

After the shoreline turned north they examined it closely, making sure that each bay was closed at its eastern end. This led to both ships running aground one night. They were refloated on the rising tide without damage, since the bottom was all mud. The coxswain was blamed for the mishap. His duties included sounding to measure the depth of water.

The next day was June 12. As *Sutil* and *Mexicana* sailed north they saw two ship's boats under sail travelling along the shore. Since they had seen lights two nights earlier as they sailed across the mouth of a bay, they presumed correctly that the boats belonged to the English ships about which they had heard from *"nuestro amigo Tetacus."* That night they sailed on until two o'clock in the morning, then anchored in five fathoms sand, not wanting to go on the mud again.

Daylight came soon. To the west they could see Narvaez's Isla de Cepeda; a low marshy coastline extended to the east of it in an unbroken line. Thus the Isla de Cepeda became the Punta de Cepeda and one entrance to the Canal de Floridablanca disappeared from the map. The new name disappeared a little later; the English called it Point Roberts.

A boat was launched, which followed the shoreline as closely as possible to make absolutely sure there was no opening, while the schooners crept along under reduced sail. When it was certain that the shore was continuous, the ships went about and made sail so as to round the point and see what lay to the north.

At seven next morning a brigantine flying the English flag was seen. She came up astern of *Sutil* and after an exchange of salutes her commander asked permission to lower a boat. Galiano replied, expressing the pleasure this would give him, and with this exchange of courtesies the first meeting between the officers of the Spanish and English navies took place on board *Sutil*. It was the thirteenth day of June 1792 (at least that was the date on board *Sutil*). On the English ship it was June 14.[1] The English had sailed by way of Cape of Good Hope, New Holland (Australia), Tahiti, and the Sandwich (Hawaiian) Islands. There was no international date line in those days and the English were using a local time about sixteen hours ahead of European time while the Spaniards were using about eight hours behind. I say "about" because there was of course no standard time zone either, and the commander of each expedition used a ship's time which put the sun somewhere near the meridian at noon.

The brigantine was *Chatham* and its commander was *"Teniente de la Marina Inglesa Guillermo Roberto Broughton."* It says something for the narrator that he was able to get Lieutenant Broughton's surname right, but when Broughton told them that his superior officer in the corvette *Discovery* was *"Capitan Jorge Vancower"* the narrator slipped a little. Broughton and Galiano told each other of their voyages and their discoveries. Galiano told Broughton that Quadra was at Nootka awaiting Vancouver.

Broughton proposed that the two expeditions should join forces and said there was a good supply of water in the bay to the south where *Discovery* lay at anchor, and where Vancouver would be pleased to offer all the facilities at his command to Galiano. Galiano expressed his gratitude and agreed to join Vancouver if wind and weather permitted. Broughton then returned to his ship and sailed off to the west around the Punta de Cepeda. It was two o'clock in the afternoon before Galiano's ships could make it around the point.

What did all this courteous exchange mean? It has been suggested that it was a camouflage for mutual suspicion and distrust and that Galiano wanted no part of any joint effort with Vancouver.[2] I believe the probabilities and the evidence did not indicate this at all. Here were two competent seamen; Galiano had been at sea for seventeen years, three years of which were on the current voyage while Vancouver had been at Nootka with Cook fourteen years earlier. They met, as we shall see later on, at the furthest extent of European exploration and exchanged maps and navigational data. They did work in company for a time, and parted for the announced reason that the English ships could not be risked in the small channels explored by the Spanish ones, and the little *Sutil* and *Mexicana* could not keep up with the much larger *Discovery* and *Chatham* in open water. Certainly, *Chatham* showed her stern to *Sutil* on June 13th.

Motives are hard enough to gauge in any case, and even harder if all one has is a set of documents nearly two hundred years old, but I prefer to think that the friendship was genuine. Certainly I have found nothing in the documents to suggest otherwise.

Galiano finally rounded the Punta de Cepeda and tried to trace the shoreline to the north, but ran into turbid water and a strong current which carried him out to sea. This was, of course, the freshet discharge of the Fraser River. The breeze was blowing from the shore, so the oars were put to use to try and row against the current. The men had done a lot of rowing in the last few days and were tired out. It is no easy job to move a forty-five ton ship against the wind by means of oars. Finally, the commanders abandoned the attempt and sailed across to the other side of the Gulf where they anchored offshore in fifteen fathoms sand, with a clear bottom and three fathoms depth almost to the shoreline. The "clear bottom" was important, since the anchor cables were made of hemp and could chafe through and break if they were entangled in rocks.

The anchorage was between two points, a situation which could be dangerous with an onshore breeze, since the ships could make very little progress to windward even under good conditions, and lost ground when they were put about. At daylight, Vernaci was sent off in the launch to the north to look for a sheltered anchorage. The northeast wind picked up strength and four hours after Vernaci left they still saw no sign of him. Just as Galiano decided he must get out of there and make for Porlier Pass, which Narvaez had shown on his map, the launch came into view. On reaching his ship Vernaci reported that there was no anchorage within two leagues. Both ships made sail in a hurry and headed up the coast. By noon they were off an entry which Galiano decided was Narvaez's "Bocas de Porlier." As they ran in under the shelter of the point the wind died, but the current carried them into the entry. There was no sign of a beach and no likely looking spot to anchor, and Galiano was concerned about getting involved in a maze of small low islands which lay inside. Suddenly, a squall hit *Mexicana* and she almost capsized. It was time to get out, so again the men took to the oars.

Getting out of a tidal channel is not as easy as getting in. The current was stronger, the wind fell light, and it took two hours of labour at the oars to get clear of the entry and make sail. *Mexicana* managed to squeeze past the windward point of an island in the entry. The rocks on the bottom were clearly seen, but the keel passed over them without striking. *Sutil*, says the narrator, preferred to pass between the island and the shore, a manoeuvre which happily was successful.

Unfortunately for the narrator we have a copy of the formal report of this incident to the Viceroy, signed by Galiano and Valdés.[3] According to this report *Sutil* was caught in an eddy and came out stern first. It is not easy to imagine that Galiano "preferred" this method of clearing the pass.

By this time the wind had veered and was now blowing from the east, so they were able to sail on easily up the coast, heading for the Bocas de Winthuysen, which appeared on Narvaez's map. A mile beyond the point at the entrance to Winthuysen they anchored in a sheltered bay which they named Cala del Descanso, or Bay of Rest. It is still called Descanso Bay.

Rest they badly needed. The toil and danger of the last four days had exhausted the whole crew. However, those days had also enabled them to correct the mistakes and extend the knowledge of previous voyages, which in the view of the narrator more than made up for the labour and fatigue. If Luis Galvez and his nameless shipmates expressed their views the record can no longer be found.

The Indians at the Cala del Descanso were nervous and diffident, but not hostile. They offered sardinas to their visitors and were willing to trade woolen cloaks made of dog hair. The dogs, white in colour and many of them shorn, could be seen in large numbers around the village. Pieces of iron were much in demand, also abalone shells from Monterey and beads.

While the men were busy filling water casks and carrying them off to the ship the officers had an opportunity to bring their charts and calculations up to date. The narrator also organized and expanded his notes on all the events of the voyage, since the rough jottings made at sea might be confusing to the reader. If we believe this passage, it indicates that the narrative was written and edited at quiet intervals during the voyage.

After a few days the crew was rested, the water casks were full, firewood supplies were replenished, but the wind was from the east, which was where they wanted to go. The commanders ordered sail anyway and the goletas spent all day trying to work eastward across the Gulf to the Punta de Lángara to the north of the Punta de Cepeda. It was now realized that Lángara was not an island. The Canal de Floridablanca was disappearing from the map. Ironically the Spanish prime minister of that name was also disappearing. He was headed for prison, the usual reward then given to former prime ministers by their successors. *Sutil* and *Mexicana* sailed all night. A loud bang signalled the first recorded collision with a floating log in the Gulf, but there was no damage and the next morning they anchored off the Punta de Lángara.

The Indians came off in canoes. They were a lively, cheerful and good natured bunch, so the sailors elected to teach them to sing *"el Malbourg."* I know the song. Malbourg was the Duke of Marlborough and the song was originally French:

Malbourg s'en va-t-en guerre
Malbourg s'en va-t-en guerre
Malbourg s'en va-t-en guerre
Dieu sait qu'il reviendra.

I don't know how this song got into the repertory of the San Blas Opera and Sailing Society, but we are piling up the "firsts." This is the first recorded performance in British Columbia of the tune to which service clubs now put the words "For he's a jolly good fellow."

After the singing was finished and the sea birds had presumably settled down again, the sun set and they passed a quiet night apart from the anchor watch on *Sutil* who had to work with the rudder and an oar to clear the ship from a large log drifting down onto their anchor cable.

114

At seven in the morning of June 21 a ship's boat came in view and the oarsmen altered course towards the anchorage.[4] As expected it turned out to be a boat from the English ships, and "Mr. Vancower" was on board. He was returning to his ships which were still anchored some miles to the south, after exploring the nearby waters. He had just named the Canal de Sasamat "Burrard's Inlet." He had left on his boat expedition before Galiano and Broughton met, so it was the first he knew of the presence of the Spanish explorers. The courtesies were less elaborate this time; Galiano simply invited Vancouver aboard and gave him breakfast. The offer to join forces was repeated and received with thanks, but since there was a flat calm there was nothing much that could be done about it. Vancouver set off, duly fed, and Galiano sent Salamanca and Vernaci off in their boats to have another look at the inlet which Vancouver had explored the week before.

This has been cited as evidence that Galiano did not trust Vancouver, but I prefer my own opinion that Galiano could hardly report back to the Viceroy that he had been *told* there was no entrance to the North west Passage in the place which was, in the Viceroy's view, the most likely if not the only possible location for it. Besides, Vancouver had said that he did not explore an arm of the inlet which lay to the north of its inner end. Anyway, off went Vernaci and Salamanca in the boats and what is now Vancouver Harbour received its second set of European visitors in a week. It was to be many years before another European would visit the place.

What did these young veterans of a voyage half way around the world have to say about their visit to the harbour? The narrator did not go along, so he recorded what they told him on their return.

There was not such an agreeable view anywhere with such diversity of trees and tender plants, neither such graceful flowers and beautiful fruits nor such a variety of animals and birds; and if the ear should tire of their music the observer could admire the prodigious mass of the mountains clothed with pines and crowned with snow melting into spectacular cascades which reach the end of their careers at an enormous speed, breaking the silence of these solitary retreats. The reunited streams from these cascades watered the plants along their banks and provided a home for the spawning salmon. When men were encountered, although differing in appearance and colour from the Spaniards, there was no doubt they were of the same species and similar inclination. It was seen that, without the conveniences the observer believed essential to live, these men kept themselves healthy, strong, and happy; and even without that help which is the fruit of study and of perfection of the arts they knew how to secure the right sustenance, satisfy their needs, and defend themselves from their enemies.

There was no entrance to the Northwest Passage.

Before Salamanca and Vernaci had finished reporting this a light easterly breeze had sprung up and the goletas weighed anchor and sailed westwards along the northern shore. It was the morning of June 25. During the afternoon Vancouver's ships came into sight to the south and both commanders altered course to join company. Galiano and Valdés spent most of the afternoon with Vancouver aboard *Discovery*. Acording to an account of Vancouver's voyage, Galiano told the English officers that the Indians had informed his people that there was a channel to the northwest, leading to the sea.[5] Vancouver admired the ability of the Spaniards to speak the native language but did not give much weight to the Indians' story. All night the little fleet sailed along the coast, although the Spanish ships had difficulty keeping up with the English ones. Galiano did not stop to examine two of the inlets he passed during this time. He had a favouring breeze, he was sailing in company with Vancouver and Broughton, and they had told him they had explored the full length of these inlets.

The next night *Discovery* reported she had found a place where the anchor would hold, so the four ships closed up. "We let go the anchor," says the narrator, "in twenty-six fathoms gravel to the south of an island we later named Quema. *Mexicana,* closer to the shore, found thirty-six fathoms half a cable away, and there anchored."

Interlude

PLACE NAMES

Names can be a tricky business. It is just as well for Galiano that the Canal de Floridablanca disappeared. If he had gone back to Spain bearing a map showing a prominent geographical feature named for the jailed ex-prime minister he might have fallen under suspicion. Even as it was, his career was stalled for a year or two simply because he had served under Malaspina who was then in prison.

The Viceroy of New Spain was a safe bet. New Spain at that time included all the coast of the Gulf of Mexico from Florida west, as well as the Caribbean Islands and Central America. The Viceroy's name was just as impressive as his realm. He was Juan Vicente de Guemes Pacheco de Padilla Horcacitas y Aguayo, Conde de Revilla Gigedo. This provided enough names to look after a good long strip of coast plus some offshore islands without taking into consideration that he was also Baron and Territorial Lord of the manors and barony of Bellinoba and Rivarroy, Knight Commander of the Order of Calatrava, Gentleman of His Majesty's Chamber, and several more lines of script.[1]

As Galiano worked his way up the coast, naming everything in sight, Vancouver was doing the same thing, bestowing names as he went. Since Spain withdrew from the scene a few years later, only a few of the names given by the Spanish have stayed in place. We have mentioned San Juan Islands and Descanso Bay. There are others: Texada Island, Cape Lazo, and the Ballenas Islands. Some have been modified, and some shifted, like Fidalgo, whose name was removed from an inlet and applied to one of the islands bordering it. Presumably because of the presence of a large number of gulls, Narvaez named a point Punta de Gaviota. The letters "v" and "b" are really the same in Spanish and this became Gabiota, Gabiola, and then Gabriola. By that time it was known to be an island, and it is now Gabriola Island. The Bocas de Porlier is still Porlier Pass, but the islands on either side of it were named Galiano and Valdés by Captain Richards of the Royal Navy. He is the person who gave us most of the Spanish place names which are the only remnant of the time when the west coast of Canada was La Costa Septentrional.

We have something more than the bare place names, thanks to Captain John Walbran, who was engaged in marine surveys on the coast of British Columbia from 1891 to 1903. Walbran was an expert navigator and surveyor and his book *British Columbia Coast Names* published in 1909 shows his familiarity with both Spanish and English documents. It is also excellent reading.

Among the Spanish and English names there is a sprinkling of presumed Indian ones. Nootka, which Cook thought was an Indian place name, is one of these. He thought the Indians were telling him the name of their village. It is a classic case of misunderstanding. There are a number of versions of the story of Captain Cook's arrival which show a high degree of consistency, although there are minor differences as is always the case with oral history. Here it is, as told by Winnifred David:[2]

> They started talking Indian, and they told (Cook) to go around the Sound. They started making signs and they were talking Indian and they were saying *Nu-tka-(k)ichim, nu-tka(k)ichim* they were saying. That means go around the harbour. So Captain Cook said, Oh, they're telling us the name of this place is "Nootka, Nootka." But the Indian name is altogether different. So it's called Nootka now and (on) the whole of the West Coast we're all Nootka Indians now.

12

THE NARROW WATERS

The anchorage south of Quema Island was exposed to winds and currents, but none of the four ships had any difficulty during the first night. The next day dawned clear, and Vancouver proposed to Galiano that three boat expeditions should be sent out to explore the various openings that can be seen from Kinghorn Island, as we call it. Galiano suggested that he should send Valdés to the northeast while the English directed their attention to the other channels. This agreed, off went Valdés, while Broughton headed northwest, and Puget took the opening to the southwest.[1] Broughton soon returned to report that there was a better anchorage for the ships in the inlet he was exploring, then left again.

Vancouver and Galiano went ashore with the artificial horizon and instruments to fix the latitude. The two navigators differed only by 20 seconds in their calculations.

The work of Vancouver and Galiano came to a sudden end in a southerly squall. *Discovery* and *Mexicana* dragged their anchors. *Chatham* took off under bare poles, and *Sutil* under reefed topsails. The wind was blowing towards the shore, the four ships with different sailing characteristics were close together, and two of them were dragging. However, with some difficulty, they slowly gained control and all moved to the anchorage that had been reported by Broughton.

Valdés got back to his ship just before dark. He had followed his assigned inlet to its end without seeing anyone. In an abandoned village he found a board covered with painted figures, so he called the inlet Brazo de la Tabla. Somehow this got changed to Toba, and so it remains. He told Broughton the inlet was closed, but Broughton went in to have a look anyway.

Here the narrative becomes a bit testy. The Spaniards complained to Vancouver who said he had perfect confidence in them but was under instructions to survey all the inlets himself. Since Vancouver was the one who had proposed they join forces it is understandable that Valdés was annoyed. It seems to have blown over; at any rate they all continued their explorations in the ships' boats and copied each other's maps. As a

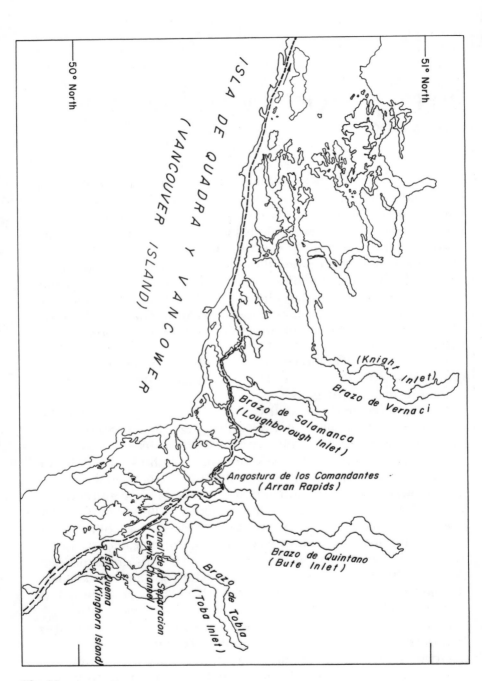

The Narrow waters.

matter of fact, Galiano's instructions were to let the English see his maps but not to let them make copies.[2] By this time the practical advantages of collaboration outweighed the political considerations.

It was at this anchorage that the tide was seen to rise and fall without perceptible currents except for occasional wind-driven ones. This, said the narrator, reminded him of a place in the Strait of Magellan where the tide could rise and fall five fathoms with no current at all. The reason was, of course, the same in the two places. The tide comes in at both ends of an inlet and somewhere in the middle the two tide streams meet and the water just rises and falls. The narrator makes no comment but I think he knew already that to the north there must have been an opening to the sea, just as the Indians said. It is not an important point, because two weeks later Broughton returned from a boat expedition to the westward to report that there was a channel leading north to the sea, and that it was suitable for ships to use. To Broughton, then, goes the honour of proving incontrovertibly that the mass of land which had been on their port hand as they worked north was an island. It is fitting that Vancouver and Broughton were the first to arrive at Nootka with the news.

Vancouver decided to back-track and follow the newly discovered channel. It appears there was some flexibility in his instructions after all. Galiano decided to continue the painstaking work of exploring the narrow channels he and his officers had seen on their boat expeditions. Thus did the two explorers part.

Sutil and *Mexicana* worked their way slowly north. The first day (July 13) they tacked back and forth and ended up back where they started. The next day was no better; the ships made half a mile of progress to windward and lost it on the last two tacks. After several days, they made it through the channel to more open water by furling the sails and rowing. Under the same conditions I have beat through the Canal de la Separación (Lewis Channel) in three hours, without asking my crew to row. It took them five days.

They continued under oars, giving each night's anchorage a name: Cevallos, Robredo, Murphy, Concha. Murphy? Yes indeed, Murphy. Jacobo Murphy, like the others named, was one of Malaspina's officers and therefore a former shipmate. Galiano did not confine himself to shipmates. He named one channel the Canal de Carvajal in tribute to *"nuestro amigo Don Ciriaco Gonzalez Carvajal"* to whom their commission was much indebted. This was a good idea. Carvajal was the Viceroy's judge auditor in Mexico. At the end of a voyage the commander had to give an accounting for all the stores and equipment placed in his ship. If this did not satisfy the *oidor* the commander had to pay for the shortages out of his own pocket. The narrator did not bring out this point in the *Relación,* contenting himself with a reference to unspecified *"particulares servicios"* by Carvajal.

Just ahead of the Anclage de Concha lay the Angostura de los Comandantes, so named because this narrows had been reconnoitred by the two commanders while the ships lay at the Anclage de Murphy. It was and is a fearsome place. The *Sailing Directions for British Columbia* say this of the Arran Rapids:

> Strong tidal streams and, at times, violent eddies and whirlpools exist in parts of Cordero Channel. These streams reach maximum velocities ... of 9 knots in the Arran Rapids. The duration of slack water is very brief, usually not more than 5 minutes. Local weather and the amount of land drainage can affect the turn of the stream, which at times can be abrupt with no period of dead slack water .... Due to the strength of the tidal streams and the turbulence that develops navigation should not be attempted other than at or near slack water.

The force of the current, which the Spaniards overestimated at twelve knots, was only part of the problem. The passage is shallow and winding, and contains numerous rocks and holes. This is the cause of the whirlpools, overfalls, and violent eddies which the commanders were able to see for themselves, and this is the nature of the channel the Spaniards proposed to negotiate, without charts or tidal publications. The Indians of a nearby village warned them against attempting the passage, but said if the ships must attempt it they should get under way when the sun reached a certain high mountain. The Spaniards thanked their hosts for the advice and for the gift of fresh salmon and herring which accompanied it.

It was observed that when the flood was running against them in the Angostura an eddy ran in their favour along the western shoreline where the ships were anchored. Canadian Tidal Publication No. 23 shows this eddy, exactly as described in the *Relación*. At three o'clock in the afternoon the flood began to slacken and the oars were ordered out with the intention of reaching a cove they could see through the rapids on the right side. *Mexicana* dropped anchor in the cove but *Sutil* caught the first of the ebb and was carried past; now in mid channel, now up against the rocky shore, completely out of control. *Sutil,* all forty-five tons of her, spun around in a whirlpool three times, so fast that the sailors were dizzy; then they used the oars as poles to push her along the shore. *Mexicana* decided to follow. *Sutil* broke a cable trying to make fast to the rocks, but after a while both ships reached another cove, or perhaps were carried there by hazard.

The beauties of nature were lost on the narrator that night. The wind whistled through the trees and the roaring of the waters surging past the ships was more terrifying than anything encountered in the whole voyage including the dismasting of *Mexicana* in the gale on the voyage north from Acapulco. The perils of the shore.

The next day was July 21st. The season was getting on and there were a lot of unknown waters between them and Nootka. More rapids lay ahead, with dangers similar to those in the Angostura de los Comandantes, plus added turbulence caused by several small islands in the channel. The wind was blowing so hard against them that the ships had to miss the morning slack although the boats were able to get through to inspect the rapids and return to report finding an anchorage on the other side. The next morning the wind dropped for a while but the flood was running against them.

Early in the evening the current slackened and although there were still some gusts of wind blowing down the channel Galiano ordered an attempt to pass the rapids. *Mexicana* was closer to the narrows (Dent Rapids) and with hard rowing she made it to the anchorage on the other side. The eddies strengthened and in spite of equally hard rowing *Sutil* could not get around the point. The backwash carried her on to a shoal and the crew had to abandon rowing and use the oars to push her off. Fortunately, the fourth and last attempt landed *Sutil* back where she started. The current might have caught her and shot her in almost any direction.

Galiano was a quick study and early the next morning he had his crew back at the *malditos* oars. He crept along the shore as the current slackened and the next thing they knew they were around the point, past the rapids and sailing along past *Mexicana*. Valdés got the anchor in and soon joined *Sutil,* so there they all were peacefully bowling along at the usual four knots as if there had been no danger at all.

The ships now entered a channel containing the usual canoes full of friendly Indians, who advised the Spaniards that the opening to the sea lay to the northwest. *Sutil* and *Mexicana* promptly turned towards the *northeast*. The Indians did not understand the procedure of tacking against the wind and retired to the shore since their advice was apparently being ignored.

With the rapids behind them, the explorers had an easier time. It was a matter of perseverance, moving the ships ahead when wind and current were favourable and anchoring while the two pilots, Salamanca and Vernaci, went off exploring one inlet after another in the boats. This is plain hard, useful work but most of it is unexciting. On one expedition Vernaci tried to take a short cut back to his ship, but the channels among the islands at the mouth of Knight Inlet are something like the streets in the old quarter of Madrid; it's pretty hard to tell where they are leading.

In the end he got lost and had to back-track and return by the same route he had taken from his ship. Since he had taken provisions for only a few days the commanders were greatly relieved when he showed up safe and sound. The Indians were not happy about this expedition; they came out in their canoes and showed Vernaci both otter skins and bows and arrows. Probably this meant, "If you're not here to trade stagger off." They tried to restrain Vernaci from entering some of the inlets but he persevered and in the end there was no trouble.

These explorations by boat could not be carried out with any great accuracy. The explorers had no time to make proper surveys, and could get a latitude observation only occasionally. I think it probable that the only surveying instrument available in the boats was a compass. The twists and turns of the fjords are shown on the Spanish maps, but distances are far from accurate and may have been only estimates based on the time it took to row from one point to the next, with or against a tidal current of unknown force.

Vancouver's maps suffer from the same limitations, although he could do more work with his larger ships and crews and his officers seem to have been better at "eyeball" measurements than the Spaniards.

One day, while the ships were anchored, there occurred the first case of occupational illness in British Columbia. Moisture had got into the mercury used in the artificial horizons and after trying a number of methods of getting rid of this, it was decided to boil the mercury in a pot. A man "of fifty years" was sent ashore to do this. Did it cross Galiano's mind that this decidedly ancient mariner was the least useful and therefore most expendable member of the crews? At any rate, while the *anciano* was stirring the pot he became afflicted with pains and began to run a fever and sweat copiously. The outcome was successful; the mercury was rid of its moisture and restored to its original purity. The man also recovered from his bout of mercury poisoning.

As the ships made their way to the northwest the channels became wider and wider and the gulf we call Queen Charlotte Sound opened up ahead of them. August was fast wearing away and they were pinned down by rain and adverse winds for twelve days. When the weather improved it was decided to break off the exploration and head for Nootka.

A few days later the commanders realized the ships were close to the point they called Cabo Scot. They anchored out in thirty fathoms to be ready for an attempt to round the Cape in the morning.

A tense moment at the end of the Canal de Salamanca (now Loughborough Inlet.) The "suspicious pursuit" by the Indians ended peaceably. Courtesy Museo Naval de Madrid.

Interlude

QUADRA AT NOOTKA

Quadra made good use of his time at Nootka. Moziño and his assistants were busy with their scientific observations and Quadra cultivated the friendship of Maquinna, but there was a lot more to do. First, Galiano's ships had to be refitted and sent on their way, as recounted in an earlier chapter.

On July 4 an English frigate came in to Nootka.[1] This was *Daedelus* which carried supplies and instructions for Vancouver. Its commander was Thomas New, who had replaced "Ricardo Agusto" (Richard Hergest) when he was killed by Hawaiians. New carried a letter signed by Floridablanca, Prime Minister of Spain.[2] It directed whoever was in command at Nootka to immediately put the bearer of the letter in possession of the buildings and lands which were occupied by British subjects in April 1789.

This must have put Quadra in a quandary. It was quite different to his instructions from the Viceroy. The "buildings" occupied by Meares had been torn down even before April 1789 and the "lands" might mean anything from the site of Meares' camp to the whole coast of America north of San Francisco. Quadra was able to convince New that the best thing to do was to wait for Vancouver, so they settled down amiably to do this. They could not know, of course, that Floridablanca was by that time in prison. Quadra's decision to follow the Viceroy's instructions was a fortunate one.

Sixteen ships put in at Nootka during the summer. Most of them were English or American traders, although Viana arrived in a Portuguese ship. He had been the nominal captain of *Ifigenia* in 1789 and he told Quadra she had carried Portuguese colours at that time. Quadra took depositions from anyone who had been at Nootka in 1789. The Americans, as well as Viana, supported Martinez and denied that Meares had any standing. This proves that they disliked Meares and Colnett, but perhaps not much more.

A more serious question arose with the arrival of a Captain William Brown in the English ship *Butterworth*. He had two other ships under command and carried some sort of permission from London to establish three "factories" or trading posts, one in the Queen Charlotte Islands and two on the mainland. Brown had come by way of Cape Horn, leaving a sealing crew at the Isla de Los Estados (Staten Island) off the Atlantic coast of Tierra del Fuego. The *Butterworth* squadron was in trouble as soon as it arrived. Brown anchored first in Clayoquot Sound and got into a quarrel with Wikaninish, the chief. This resulted in the deaths of three Indians, one of them the chief's brother. Wikaninish appealed to Quadra for help in a mission of vengeance. Quadra could not do this, and had some difficulty in dissuading a group of chiefs from attacking Brown. Quadra's support of Brown, who moved to Nootka soon after, cost him the friendship of the Indians for a time, but after a while things were patched up. Brown was by then absorbed in an unsuccessful attempt to forbid American traders to operate on the Coast.[3]

Quadra had started the season with an imposing fleet. He had brought *Santa Gertrudis* and the schooner *Activa* from San Blas to Nootka, where *Concepción* had been since 1790. He had Caamaño in *Aranzazu* off exploring to the north and Fidalgo standing by at Nuñez Gaona. He decided there were too many mouths to feed and a show of force was unnecessary so on July 18 he ordered *Santa Gertrudis* to return to San Blas, and on its way to look in on Fidalgo in the Strait of Juan de Fuca. If Fidalgo was not at Nuñez Gaona he could be found at some other port in the Strait.[4] This is the only mention I have found of a possible settlement at some other place in the Strait.

Quadra also told Eliza to rig *Concepción* for sea and return to San Blas, taking with him Alberni and the surviving members of the Company of Catalonian Volunteers. Since they had all been at Nootka for over two years I imagine this order was obeyed with enthusiasm.

This left Quadra at Nootka with one schooner, its crew, and Moziño and his two assistants. He does not seem to have had any qualms about the size of Vancouver's squadron nor about the growing incidence of violence between traders and Indians.[5]

Quadra's trust in the native people was not undermined by the death of Pedro Santa Ana and his men in 1775. Ths only other violent incident in which he had been involved was a confused clash at Bucareli Sound in 1779 during which one or two Indians died before peace was restored.[6] His trust was justified. There was no violence by or against Spaniards at any time during this last visit by Quadra to the country for which they had no name.

127

13

THE COMMISSIONERS

Less than two days after *Sutil* and *Mexicana* arrived at Nootka they were under way again, headed for Monterey. During this time Quadra changed his strategy for his commission with Vancouver. Throughout the summer Quadra intended to deliver Nootka to the English. He had sent his two frigates south, and with them most of the guns from the fort at the entrance to the harbour.[1] His first letter to Vancouver, dated August 29, before Galiano's arrival, offered to turn over the whole establishment to Vancouver while he removed himself to "Fuca" (he didn't say Nuñez Gaona) to set up a Spanish establishment there.

During the next few days several things happened. Galiano had arrived with two reports, the first confirming that Nuñez Gaona was not safe from winter gales, and the second that there was no Northwest Passage. At the same time Vancouver replied to Quadra's letter on September 1 Vancouver time or August 31 Quadra time, saying it was his view that everything north of San Francisco came under the condominium provisions of the Nootka Convention but that he (Vancouver) was there only to take delivery of the English land and buildings.

Warren Cook takes the view that the unsuitability of Nuñez Gaona was the significant factor in Quadra's change of plan.[2] I doubt this, because Quadra knew about the problems of Nuñez Gaona through reports from Fidalgo on July 22, after Galiano's visit, and Galiano sent along his own negative report on Nuñez Gaona with Vancouver.[3] Quadra was also uncertain whether Fidalgo was at Nuñez Gaona or some other port in "Fuca" when he sent *Santa Gertrudis* south in July.[4]

My view is that the significant report was the one about the Northwest Passage, although Caamaño did not return from still more searches farther north until September 8. In Eliza's opinion the only possible location was through the Strait of Juan de Fuca and this seems to have been accepted. The Viceroy's instructions laid great stress on the Northwest Passage and on the importance of informing him as soon as anything about it was discovered.

Vancouver's letter eliminated any chance of carrying out the Viceroy's instructions. I suggested earlier that this chance was almost non-existent right from the start. Quadra decided to stall the negotiations until he could get new instructions from the Viceroy which meant the next year. My reasons are conjectural but the shift in Quadra's strategy is not. The documents demonstrate it.

The commissioners were hampered by the absence of either a common tongue or an interpreter. A Mr. Dobson, who was one of the officers of *Daedalus,* understood some Spanish and acted as a translator of letters between the two commissioners. This slowed things down, especially when Dobson hurt his arm and could not write for several days. There is a minor mystery here. Galiano and Vancouver had little difficulty in understanding each other, as their separate accounts of the same events show. Vancouver and Quadra understood each other well enough to become good friends. One suspects that Quadra's caution with written documents was part of his delaying tactics, and that this inspired a corresponding caution in Vancouver.

Vancouver's instructions told him only to take possession of the "land and buildings" at Nootka and at nearby Port Cox which were occupied by British subjects in April 1789. He must have realized soon after his arrival that there was no land occupied by anyone at that time, nor were there any buildings, Meares' hut having been torn down when he left in 1788.[5]

The exchange of letters went something like this:[6]

Quadra: There is really nothing to restore. I have some depositions from the Americans, who say there was no British subject or property here in April 1789.

Vancouver: I have some depositions from Colnett's people. My job is to take over the whole port when you are ready to leave. No hurry.

Quadra: Our *establecimiento* isn't even on the site used by Meares. We'd be glad to cede you his camp area at the end of the beach.

Vancouver: Sorry, that's not enough. My instructions don't permit me to negotiate.

Quadra: If you'll recognize the Strait of Juan de Fuca as the boundary I'll let you have all of Nootka.

Vancouver: I'm not authorized to discuss that. The whole port must have been what was intended by our masters.

This sterile exchange did not hamper social intercourse.

Quadra: Dine with me.[7]

Vancouver: A pleasure. I'll bring the drinks.

Quadra:	Let's go to Tahsis and visit Maquinna. He makes a good porpoise and tuna stew by throwing hot rocks in a trough of water with the whole fish, guts and all. I'd like you to meet him.[8]
Vancouver:	Good idea. What should I take as a gift?

The friends seemed to enjoy this, but autumn was upon them, so finally they agreed to leave business matters to be settled between Madrid and London and headed south.

Meanwhile, Galiano and Valdés were well down the coast. They had a look at the Entrada de Heceta, now called the Columbia River, but did no more than satisfy themselves that the lay of the land fitted the description given by *"el activo navegante americano,* Mr. Gray," when he had entered it a few months earlier. Gray had exchanged ships with Kendrick and was in command of the *Columbia* when he named the river after his ship. Galiano sent his dispatches on to Mexico by other ships from Monterey and lingered in the sunshine there until October 22nd. *Sutil* and *Mexicana* then weighed anchor for the last time on the voyage and the crew made sail. There was one last tussle with the weather. *Mexicana* almost capsized in a gale and this time *Sutil* was driven away and lost touch with her consort for the first time on the voyage. However Valdés was able to repair the damage to *Mexicana*. He and Galiano arrived at Acapulco on November 23, 1792, six and a half months after their departure.

The narrator then picked up his pen to write the last entry in the journal.

> *Terminado el objeto con que se habian habilitado estos buques, los entregamos al Oficial Comandante del Departmento, y nos preparamos para regresar a Europa por la via de Mexico y Vera Cruz.* (Having achieved the objective for which these vessels were fitted out, we turned them over to the Commanding Officer of the Department and prepared ourselves to return to Europe by way of Mexico and Vera Cruz.)

14

NOOTKA ABANDONED

On Quadra's departure, Fidalgo took charge of the establecimiento at Nootka. Fidalgo was highly suspicious of Indians and seems to have been trigger-happy. During the summer one of his officers had walked off alone from the stockade at Nuñez Gaona and his body was found a few days later. When this was reported to Fidalgo, without any enquiry he opened fire on the two canoes which happened to be nearest and killed nearly everyone in them. This earned him a stiff reprimand from Quadra and in due course further reprimands from the Viceroy and even from the King.[1] Fidalgo did not repeat his mistake, but he did keep the Indians out of the establecimiento at Nootka, to the puzzlement of Maquinna, who had told Vancouver he was distressed at the thought that the Spanish might leave. However, before the winter was out, Fidalgo had to soften his attitude. Some of the vegetables in the garden were destroyed by an early frost and during the winter a lot more were damaged by the damp which got into the storehouse. The same damp ruined part of the stock of flour.[2] With many of his men down with scurvy Fidalgo was only too glad to see Maquinna when he came in the early spring with gifts of fish and game. The Spaniards were better at observing fishing and hunting methods used by the Indians than at catching their own food.

While Fidalgo was suffering through his first northern winter his superiors in Mexico and Madrid were trying to hammer out a policy for the northern coast. The first of the many documents that kept the scribes busy that winter was a whole sheaf of letters sent to the Viceroy by Quadra from Monterey, all dated October 24, 1792.[3]

Quadra was apparently much impressed by the number of ships of various nationalities which had visited Nootka during the summer. He was worried by the presence of the *Butterworth* squadron and mentioned both in his journal and in his letters that they had already formed an establishment on the Isla de los Estados.[4] Why he should have been so concerned about this I do not know. The Isla de los Estados is an island lying off the Atlantic coast of Tierra del Fuego. There is no question that Quadra knew which island he was talking about; he gave its latitude and longitude in his journal. Perhaps he regarded this as evidence that Brown of the *Butterworth* was serious in his intent to establish three factories on the coast. Quadra also told Revilla Gigedo that Brown was expecting a fifty-gun frigate to arrive in support of his venture.

Quadra considered Nootka to be the best port in the area because one could enter or leave it at any time, the climate was healthy, there were ample stands of timber, enough arable land to sustain a garrison and the natives were well disposed towards the Spanish in contrast to the *"feroces Yndios"* at the entrance of the Strait of Juan de Fuca. It is true that one of Fidalgo's officers who wandered off alone at Nuñez Gaona was killed, but there had been several such occurrences at Nootka over the years. For whatever reason, Quadra had a low opinion of "Fuca," where there was scarcely more than a miserable village or two whose inhabitants had nothing except fish to sustain themselves or to trade.

The tidal currents and variable winds of the Strait were, and still are for that matter, an impediment to sailing vessels but Quimper, Eliza, Galiano, and Vancouver had experienced no particular difficulty in navigating the Strait.

In another of the letters sent from Monterey Quadra proposed a policy to Revilla Gigedo. He recognized that it would be impossible to prevent other nations from trading along the enormously lengthy shoreline of the Coast, no matter how well Nootka was fortified nor how many warships Spain sent there. With existing naval and military strength, he could not even defend San Francisco let alone protect the coast.[5]

His proposal to Revilla Gigedo was similar to one made earlier by Martinez. It was to leave the matter in the hands of Spanish merchants. They had a competitive advantage through the availability of Mexican cloth, copper, and other minerals as well as abalone shells from Monterey. These could be traded for furs which could be sold in Canton for silver or exchanged for luxury goods without the cost of licences from the East India Company which hampered the English, or the long haul around Cape Horn which hampered both English and Americans. This would also benefit the mills and mines in Mexico and give Spain a source of supply of silver to replace dwindling production from both Mexico and Peru. In short, Quadra wanted to drive out traders from other countries by competitive pressure.

Curiously, Quadra said little about the purpose of all this activity, since he did not expect the trade to do more than bear the cost of maintaining the Nootka establishment. He didn't want to leave to foreigners "the glory of discovering unknown countries" but did not go beyond that.

Revilla Gigedo wanted none of this. His instructions to his officers earlier in the year had required the maintenance of a post somewhere in the vicinity but now he wanted to abandon Nootka and clear out. I think the change was due to the disappearance of the Northwest Passage but it may have been only the pale cast of thought that undermined his earlier resolution.

In November 1792 Godoy, the royal favourite whom I have mentioned earlier, became Prime Minister. Aranda, who had succeeded Floridablanca in that post followed his predecessor to prison.[6] Revilla Gigedo sent a long memorandum to Godoy deprecating any further activities north of San Francisco, with the possible exception of a post at the mouth of the Columbia River and an exploration of the river itself. He thought the sea otter trade would become unprofitable and the cost of maintaining Nootka too much of a drain on the Spanish treasury for any possible benefit.[7] Future exploration should be concentrated on the coast south of Juan de Fuca. This area had not been examined because on the voyage north Spanish vessels stayed out to sea and on the way south were usually too anxious to get home and too short of supplies to do any exploring.

The political relations between Spain and England were changing at this time, although Revilla Gigedo in Mexico was always several months behind on news from Spain and was not aware of this. After the formal deposition of Louis XVI in August 1792 and his execution in January 1793 England and Spain became allies in a war against the new government of France. They were anxious to clear up the Nootka mess, and quickly entered into a new Nootka Convention which settled the damages to be paid by Spain at 210,000 pesos fuertes, or Spanish dollars. The new convention made no mention of repossessing land or vacating Nootka. Fortunately for Spain, Revilla Gigedo's authorization to Quadra to offer 653,433 pesos (page 51) was not known to the English. Fitzherbert, in a letter to his Foreign Secretary grumbled because Vancouver had not accepted Quadra's offer to turn over the site of Meares' hut which would have been adequate to settle the point of honour.[8] Thus do political changes take the wind out of the sails of honest seamen. Vancouver had no such instructions and no idea of what was going on in Europe when he and Quadra met at Nootka.

In May 1793 the Spanish supply expedition arrived at Nootka. Fidalgo was no doubt relieved that Saavedra arrived to replace him so he could return to New Spain. Spanish accounts of this time are sketchy, but we are told that two of the ten people who had been left with Fidalgo had died during the winter. A third died in June. Saavedra in turn had a hard winter, and was down to half rations before fresh supplies arrived.

The Indians had also been very short of food during the winter, so Saavedra shared what he had with them. Later in the winter they returned the favour by sharing the meat of a whale they caught with Spanish help.[9] The frigate *Aranzazu* arrived in June 1794, commanded by none other than Juan Kendrick, the son of the old Boston trader. He had entered the Spanish service the year before when his father went to Hawaii where a fellow captain honoured him with a salute. Unfortunately the gunner forgot there was a ball in the gun and Kendrick *père* was killed.[10]

Back to Nootka.

A third Nootka Convention had been negotiated between England and its ally Spain. In January 1794 it was agreed that both countries would abandon Nootka, but first the point of honour must be satisfied, for which purpose Spain would send a commissioner to Nootka and England would do the same. When the two commissioners arrived the formal surrender of nobody knew what would take place. A certain Lieutenant Pierce of the Royal Marines was sent to La Coruña where he took passage to Vera Cruz for the overland journey to San Blas, hoping to catch a northbound ship to Nootka. San Blas was as far as he got in 1794.

On March 26, 1794 the greatest figure in our story ended his career. Don Juan Francisco de la Bodega y Quadra died, either at his home near San Blas or in Mexico City, a friend of Indians, English, and Americans and respected by all of them. Robert Gray of the *Columbia* even named his first born son Don Quadra Gray.

At about the same time, Godoy's brother-in-law Branciforte replaced Revilla Gigedo as Viceroy of New Spain. Of Branciforte the poet Francisco de Quevedo might have said, "De su pecho colgaban muchas cruces." His objective was simple and his policies were consistent. He wanted to get as rich as possible as soon as possible. He had no interest in New Spain, and certainly none in its remote northern limits.

Quadra's successor José Manuel de Álava was sent to Nootka to preside over the abandonment, in the expectation that an English commissioner would show up. Álava arrived in August 1794. Saavedra had received supplies and a reinforcement of nineteen soldiers in June and now turned over command to Álava. Then they all sat down to wait for the commissioner from England, but as we have seen Pierce only got as far as San Blas.

By October Álava realized there was no possibility of the commissioner arriving that year, so presumably to Saavedra's chagrin he was restored to his command and spent that last winter at Nootka. Álava departed to spend it in Monterey.

Early the next year Pierce left San Blas in *Activa,* the last ship to be built in the dockyard there. Álava joined the ship in Monterey for the voyage north to perform the last act of the brief Spanish period on the northern coast.

It was now February 1795, only twenty-one years since Perez made the first northern voyage and only twenty since Quadra's reckless thrust to Alaska in the tiny *Sonora.* In that time no small number of Spaniards had died of disease or been killed by Indians; Indians too died at the hands of Spaniards in the occasional violent episodes.

The settlement at Nootka had never been more than a mere military outpost, raising part of its own food supply to reduce the incidence of scurvy and the cost to the royal treasury. From first to last there had been no Spanish trading vessel on the coast. Such skins as were acquired became the property of the King, this also to reduce the cost to the treasury. The maps and reports had not yet been published, except for the one narrative without maps which was probably filched and somehow came to the notice of the Honourable Daines Barrington. There had not even been any serious attempt to convert the natives to Christianity and no attempt at all to dispossess them of their sovereignty over their native land, if that European concept had any meaning in the context of Indian life.

Concern over the Russians, still in Alaska, and over their possible incursion into California had been one motive but time after time the instructions to explorers had stressed the Northwest Passage which, unlike Everest, is not there.

The forces of economics were undermining the importance of the fur trade, as Revilla Gigedo expected. Competition among buyers had driven up the cost of skins and the increased supply had lowered prices in Canton. Besides, sandalwood from Fiji would soon be of more interest to the luxury trade in China. In a few years, the Americans would be the only ones still visiting the coast.

Activa arrived at Nootka on March 16. By March 23 Álava had the buildings pulled down, the guns loaded aboard ship, and finally lowered the Spanish flag. Lieutenant Pierce, R.M., went ashore and, at the site of Meares' mansion (or hut), unfurled the Union Jack he had carried around for a year. Then he took it down again and they all sailed away together, leaving the place to the Indians, and so it ended.

Ended? Well, almost. A year later Broughton, who had commanded Vancouver's consort in 1792, arrived to receive Nootka from the Spanish. No one had remembered to cancel his instructions when it was decided to send Pierce to Nootka.

The Indians brought him up to date.

The fort and anchorage in 1793, when Fidalgo was in charge. This sketch was made by Sigismund Bacstrom of the trading vessel Three Brothers which he abbreviated to "3 Bees," translated by the Spanish to Tresbes. Bacstrom annotated his sketches and used them as a basis for paintings done later. A painting made from this sketch is in the possession of Parks Canada. Courtesy British Columbia Provincial Archives, from an original drawing in their collection.

Postlude

THE ROAD TO THE EIGHTEENTH CENTURY

You get onto the interstate highway between Bellingham and the Canadian border, then turn westward on to Route 20. As you cross a bridge on to Fidalgo Island the two-century gap begins to shrink. Another bridge takes you high over the Boca de Flon, now known as Deception Pass. Half an hour or so later you are at the ferry terminal. The man in the ticket booth is genuinely glad to see you; the youth in the parking lot waits with gentle patience while you search your pockets for the ticket. Then you drive aboard and cross the Boca de Caamaño which Eliza and Galiano did not explore because it did not lead towards the Atlantic Ocean.

On the other side you land at Port Townsend, where the citizens pride themselves on their "Victorian" buildings although that long-lived monarch never ruled over this part of the world. Civic pride is laudable, but it crosses your mind that the first settlers did not arrive here until sixty years after Eliza's voyage. You skirt the Puerto de Quadra where Eliza took his ease while Narvaez explored the Gran Canal de Nuestra Señora del Rosario for him. Later you pass inland of the Bahia de Quimper unless you want to turn aside and sample some Dungeness crab. Farther along you find that the name of the Puerto de Nuestra Señora de los Angeles has been shortened to Port Angeles.

You drive on along the coast and come at last to Nuñez Gaona where Fidalgo waited for a decision from Quadra as to whether the outpost should be built. It is now called Neah Bay. The time gap is closing rapidly now. It is here that the Makah Indian Nation has established its museum, which displays a sampling of the artifacts recovered at Ozette. You can see the implements and clothing buried five centuries in the mud, which so closely match the Spanish descriptions of Nootka, including the tiny man in a mussel shell.

The grave young man at the desk is Kirk Wachendorf, and he is quite content to leave the football game on his miniature TV to talk history. He knows the legend of the first man and is interested to hear that some white writers have altered the story, substituting "beads of sweat" or "tears" for the discharge from the nose of the mother of mankind. He remarks that white people often try to tidy up the stories of his people.

Kirk says his father remembers being told of the remains of the old Spanish buildings beside a little stream that runs into the western part of the bay, the only stream entering the sea in the vicinity. It would, he says, be the logical place for Fidalgo to choose but road building and other disturbances of the land have removed any traces of the Spanish works.

At that part of the bay, the construction of a breakwater from the island which was charted by Galiano to the western shore has reduced the exposure to heavy seas but the winds still whistle into the bay in the winter, including the southwesters which blow through the gap in the mountains.

You leave Nuñez Gaona and drive south, crossing the Olympic Peninsula to the open coast, in search of the site of the fatal landing. After a long circuit around the Quinault Indian Reservation you arrive at Taholah. Pearl Baller is the Tribal Secretary of the Quinault Nation. You explain your errand to her and she decides to give you a permit to walk on the beach where Pedro Santa Ana died. She knows the story but understandably it is not a favourite one among the Quinault Indians. She says her people have no oral tradition of the affair although some of the senior citizens (she doesn't call them old people) tell stories they or their parents probably heard from white men. She warns you that the actual location of the fatal landing is uncertain.

The beach is deserted. It is closed to the public and permits are seldom granted for a visit. You can see some of the rocks that hemmed *Sonora* in at low tide and the springs still run, tracing their courses across the wide sand beach. The forest has gone, but there is a thrifty stand of young Douglas fir growing through the thick brush.

It is September. There is a morning fog which Quadra did not encounter in July 1775 but for a moment you can almost see *Sonora* and see the boat coming ashore. Something went wrong but it is pure speculation as to what it might have been. The attack was premeditated; there is little doubt of that. A crowd of hundreds of Indians was hidden in the forest. It was several hours before high water and the Indians chose exactly the right moment to leap out of their hiding places and run down the beach, which may not have been so wide then, to attack the interlopers just as they were dragging their boat ashore through the surf. The gentle breeze is from the north today so there is almost no surf, but a westerly wind would set up seas which would run right onto the beach.

It is possible, although there is no evidence, that the Spaniards failed to respond to some signal of friendship, or that they unwittingly made some signal of war, or that the chief of the tribe had only just heard of the friendly barter of the previous day and ordered it stopped, or ... there are so many possibilities. Later, Spanish officials who had never been near La Costa Septentrional would call it treachery. Quadra and Maurelle gave no opinion, they just recorded what happened.

After a little while you leave.

BIBLIOGRAPHY

The bibliography which follows contains only those works which I have used and footnoted in writing this book. Warren Cook gives a more extensive list and also discusses the difficulty of locating some of the source material. For those interested in studying the subject in depth, the following notes may be helpful.

No original account of a Spanish voyage or of life at the estableci-miento at Nootka was published at the time. The first Spanish publication was the *Relación* of the Galiano-Valdés voyage published ten years after the event, and seven years after the Spanish had withdrawn from Nootka.

I have listed this under its title, because I do not believe that the authorship has been established. The manuscript in AGN Tomo 588 which is dated in Mexico on October 18, 1793 appears to be a fair copy written by a scribe. It bears the name Dionisio Alcalá Galiano written in the same hand, and there are spelling and grammatical corrections in a different hand. It was extensively edited before being published in 1802, with material evidently added from other accounts. For example, the published version includes some remarks about the negotiations between Bodega y Quadra and Vancouver which took place after Galiano had left Nootka. Cutter has discovered a manuscript, apparently of the published version, in Cardero's handwriting. Cardero might be the editor or author, or he might have just made a copy for some reason.

The 1802 publication, or at least one copy I have seen, bears no author's name. It was republished three years later with a supplement analyzing the various estimates of latitude and longitude for some of the important points on the North American west coast. The supplement is dated 1805 and it bears the name of Espinosa y Tello who had been one of Malaspi-na's officers and was in 1805 working in the Depósito Hidrográfico, which published the work.

The text of the 1805 printing is identical with the 1802 version, including the same printing errors and the same errata sheet, as well as the same extremely long and largely irrelevant introduction devoted largely to championing the Spanish explorers and demolishing criticism by foreign historians. I have seen two copies of this.

In editing the *Relación* of the Galiano-Valdés voyage, a number of ambiguities were introduced. Sometimes it appears that the narrator is aboard one ship, sometimes the other. The narrator uses "we" in referring to Malaspina's 1791 voyage, when Galiano was in Mexico. These ambiguities do not exist in the 1793 manuscript.

The 1805 version was republished in 1958 in Madrid. The quality of the maps is not as good, and the printer corrected only some of the original printing errors, while introducing a few new ones of his own.

Two translations of the *Relación* are listed in the bibliography. Jane translated it into English in 1930, sensibly omitting nearly all the introduction. Unfortunately he made a number of mistakes which render some passages obscure. His description of the deficiencies of the ships is particularly weak. Barwick's translation is much better, and I used it to correct some mistakes of my own, but as far as I know it was not published.

The next item to appear was Moziño's *Noticias de Nutka* which ran serially in the *Gazeta de Guatemala* in 1804-05. I have not seen this publication. It was republished in Mexico in 1913; I have a copy of this. It is close to, if not identical with, the manuscript in AGN Tomo 277. Wilson's translation contains a description of the variant manuscripts of Moziño's account, and also contains illustrations, which are lacking in the 1913 publication. Apart from some minor mistakes in transcribing words of the "Nootka" (i.e. Mowachaht) language I believe Wilson did a very good job, although I am far from competent to sit in judgement on her work.

There are a number of word lists for the Mowachaht language. Cook made one which I have not used. Ingraham, who was the mate of Gray's ship in 1789, made a list [AGN Tomo 65] which Martinez included in his 1789 diary with some additions and with the English equivalents translated correctly into Spanish. Bodega y Quadra (1792) included a word list which varies slightly from Moziño's, and the Galiano-Valdés *Relación* varies slightly from both.

Other voyage accounts were published much later. The Malaspina voyage did not appear in print until 1885 after Bancroft had completed his *History of the Northwest Coast*. I do not think Martinez's diary was printed before 1964.

As I write this Freeman Tovell of Victoria, B.C. is editing the writings of Bodega y Quadra. I hope future readers of this book will add his work to the bibliography.

This is not to say that the unpublished documents were unknown when I started. The bibliography shows that many students of the period have been browsing through the unpublished manuscripts for years. I repeat the acknowledgement I made in the introduction of the help this has given me, both in tracking down primary sources and in using direct quotations given in secondary sources.

In spite of this there are some tantalizing gaps. One would like to know Perez better and one would like to know more about life ashore at Nootka, for which the records are scanty. The Russian story of their encounters with the Spaniards appears to be as thoroughly lost as Chirikov's men. *Multum adhuc restit operis.*

Archer, Christon L., 1978. "Spanish Exploration and Settlement on the Northwest Coast." In: *Sound Heritage* (7) Prov. Archives of British Columbia.

Archivo General de la Nación, Mexico, 1774-95. Various volumes (tomos.). References are to *Historia* series unless stated otherwise (AGN).

Archivo Historico Naciónal, Madrid. Various references.

Archivo de Indias, Seville. Various references.

Baird, J. E., 1956. *San Lorenzo de Nutka.* Unpublished thesis. University of California.

Baker, A. J. (translator) 1930. "Fray Benito de la Sierra's account of Hezeta's voyage." In: *Quarterly of California Historical Society* (see de la Sierra).

Barrington, Daines (translator) 1781. *Miscellanies.* (Contains a loose translation of Maurelle's Journal of 1775). London.

Bartroli, Tomás. 1960. *The Spanish establishment at Nootka Sound.* Unpublished thesis, University of British Columbia. Vancouver.

Barwick, G. F. (translator). 1911. *Voyage of Sutil and Mexicana in 1792.* Unpublished typescript, Vancouver Public Library (see *Relación.*)

Beaglehole, J. E. (editor). 1955. *Journals of James Cook.* Cambridge Press.

Begg, Alexander. 1894. *History of British Columbia.* Toronto.

Berton, Pierre. 1970. *The National Dream.* McLelland & Stewart.

de la Bodega y Quadra, J. F. "1775 to 1779." In: *Anuario, Dirección Hidrográfica,* 1865. Madrid.

———————————— 1792. *Viage a la Costa ... Septentrional.* Archivo, Ministerio des Asuntos Exteriores, Madrid.

Boit, John. 1795-6. Log of the "Union". Published 1981. Oregon Historical Society.

Caamaño Jacinto. 1792. "Diario". In: *Archivo General de la Nación.* Translation published 1938. B.C. Historical Quarterly.

de la Campa, Miguel. 1775. "Diario." Translation published 1964. In: *Journal of Explorations.* John Howell Books.

Cook, Warren. 1973. *Flood Tide of Empire: Spain and the Pacific Northwest.* Yale Press.

Cutter, D. C. 1963. "Early Spanish Artists on the Northwest Coast." In: *Pacific Northwest Quarterly,* (54).

David, Winnifred. 1978. "The Contact Period, an Oral Tradition." In: *Sound Heritage* (7) Provincial Archives of British Columbia.

Enciclopedia General del Mar, Madrid.

Fedorova, S. H. n.d. *Russian population in Alaska and California*. Translation (1973) by Pierce and Donnelly. Limestone, Kingston, Ontario.

Fisher, Robin. 1977. *Contact and Conflict*. UBC press, Vancouver.

——————— and Bumsted, 1982. (editors). See Walker.

Fleurieu, C. P. C. 1798? *Voyage d'Etienne Marchand*. Paris.

Gunther, E. 1972. *Indian life on the northwest coast*. University of Chicago.

Haswell, R. 1788-9. "Log of the Columbia." In: *Howay* 1941 q.v.

Herr, Richard. 1958. *The 18th century revolution in Spain*. Princeton.

Howay, F. W. 1941. *Voyages of the Columbia* ... Massachussetts Historical Society.

———————1973. *Trading vessels in the Maritime fur trade*. Limestone Press, Kingston, Ontario.

Ingraham, Joseph. 1790-92. *Journal of the brigantine Hope*. Published 1971. Imprint Society.

Jane, Cecil (translator.) 1930. *A Spanish voyage to Vancouver (sic) and the northwest coast of America* (Galiano's 1792 voyage). Argonaut.

Johnson, M. O. 1911. *Spanish exploration by Juan Perez*. Unpublished thesis. University of California.

Jones, O. L. 1960. *Spanish occupation of Nootka Sound*. Unpublished thesis. University of Oklahoma.

Kendrick, John. 1778 et seq. "Diary of the Washington." In: *Howay*, 1941.

Kenyon, M. A. 1972. *Naval construction and repair in San Blas*. Unpublished thesis. University of New Mexico.

Lamb, W. Kaye. 1942. "The mystery of Mrs. Barkley's Diary." In: *British Columbia Historical Quarterly*.

——————— 1984 (editor). *The Voyage of George Vancouver*. Hakluyt.

Makah Museum, 1979. Museum exhibit leaflet.

Manning, W. R. 1904. "The Nootka Sound controversy." In: *Annual Report* (1905) American Historical Association.

Marshall, J.S. 1955. *Adventure in Two Hemispheres*. Privately published.

Martinez, Esteban Jose. 1789. "Diario." In: *Colección de diarios*. Instituto Histórico de Marina. Madrid 1964.

Massip, J. 1984 *Pere d'Alberni*. Jornado d'Estudios Catalano-Americans.

Maurelle (Mourelle) Francisco. 1775. "Diario." Museo Naval, Madrid. Variant copy in AGN (see Barrington).

Moziño. 1792. *Noticias de Nutka*. Published in Gazeta de Guatemala 1804-5. Republished Mexico 1913 (see Wilson).

Museo Naval, Madrid.

Novo y Colson, Pedro, (editor). *Viaje ... de las corbetas Descubierita y Atrevida. 1789-94*. Published 1885. Madrid (Malaspina voyage).

Parkes, H. B. 1938-69 *A History of Mexico*. Houghton Mifflin.

Pethick, D. 1980. *The Nootka connection*. Douglas & McIntyre.

Plumb, J. H. 1950. *England in the eighteenth century*. Penguin.

Quadra. See: Bodega y Quadra.

Relación del viage hecho por ... Sutil y Mexicana ... 1792. Published 1802, Madrid. Republished 1958 (see Barwick & Jane). Authorship uncertain (cited as *Relación*).

Riobó, Juan. 1779. *Viage de ... Princesa y Favorita*. Archives of Santa Clara mission.

Salvá, Jaime. n.d. *Alcalá Galiano*. Madrid.

de la Sierra, Benito. 1775. *Viaje de ... Santiago* (see Baker).

Sotos Serrano, Carmen. 1982. *Pintores de la expedición de Malaspina*. Real Academia de Historia, Madrid

Thurman, M. E. 1967. *Naval Department of San Blas*. Arthur H. Clark.

Turner, N. J. and Efrat, B. S. 1982. *Ethnobotany of the Hesquiat Indians of Vancouver Island*, B.C. Provincial Museum.

Vaughan, T. et al. 1977. *Malaspina on the Northwest Coast*. Oregon Historical Society.

Wagner, H. R. 1931. "Apochryphal Voyages." *In: Proceedings of the American Antiquarian Society (10)*.

_____1933. *Spanish Explorations of the Strait of Juan de Fuca*. Fine Arts Press.

_____1936 (translator). *Journal of Tomás de Suria 1791*. Arthur H. Clark.

_____1938. "Sovereignty rights through symbolic acts." In: Pacific Historical Review.

Walbran, John. 1909. *British Columbia Coast Names*. Ottawa.

Walker, Alexander. 1982. *Voyage to the Northwest Coast of America in 1785 and 1786*. Douglas & McIntyre.

Wike, J. A. 1951. *The effect of the maritime fur trade on northwest Indian society*. Unpublished thesis. Columbia University.

Wilson, I. H. 1970 (translator). *Noticias de Nutka*. McLelland and Stewart (see Moziño).

NOTES.

Full titles are given in the bibliography.

Chapter I. The Explorers
1. Wagner, 1931.
2. Lamb.

Chapter II. The Northwest Passage
1. W. Cook, p. 10.
2. Baird.
3. Johnson.
4. Walbran, under "Estevan."
5. In: Sound Heritage.
6. Beaglehole, p. 323.

Interlude. *Un Acta de Posesion*
1. Wagner, 1938.
2. Archivo General de la Nacion, Mexico, (AGN)
   Tomo 68. References in this source are to the "Historia" series, unless stated otherwise.

Chapter III. The Fatal Landing
1. Barrington.
2. W. Cook, p. 72.
3. Baker.
4. Bibliografia del Mar.
5. Bodega, 1775.
6. de la Campa.
7. Letter to author from Bancroft Library.
8. AGN Tomo 63.
9. Bodega, 1775.
10. de la Sierra.
11. de la Campa.
12. de la Sierra.

Chapter IV. *La Costa Septentrional*
1. de la Sierra.
2. Bodega, 1775.
3. Bodega, 1775.
4. de la Sierra.
5. W. Cook, Appendix.
6. Riobo
7. e.g. W. Cook, pp. 56, 121.
8. Fedorova.
9. Archivo Historico Nacional, Madrid. (AHN)
10. AGN Tomo 68.
11. AGN Tomo 68.
12. Jones.
13. W. Cook, p. 112.
14. Bartroli.

Interlude. Chirikov's Men
1. Fedorova.
2. Wike, quoting Father Crespi's journal.
3. Beaglehole, p. 311.
4. Beaglehole, p. 1405.

Chapter V. Martinez in Command
1. Martinez.
2. Martinez.
3. W. Cook, p. 136.
4. Marshall.
5. AGN Tomo 65.
6. Marshall.

7. Wagner, 1933.
8. AGN Tomo 65.
9. AGN Tomo 65.
10. *Archivo de Indias,* quoted in Bartroli.

Interlude. The Nootka Dispute
1. e.g. Begg.
2. Herr.
3. Plumb.
4. B.C. Provincial Archives Report, 1913.
5. AGN Tomo 67.

Chapter VI. The *Establecimiento* at Nootka
1. Bartroli.
2. W. Cook, p. 291.
3. Jones.
4. Massip.
5. AGN Tomo 69.
6. AGN Tomo 69.
7. Jones.
8. Letter from Bodega y Quadra to Revilla Gigedo, Jan. 26, 1792. Copy in B.C. Provincial Archives.
9. AGN Tomo 69.
10. AGN Tomo 69.
11. Newcombe.
12. AGN Tomo 69.
13. Moziño.
14. Novo y Colson.
15. Moziño.
16. AGN Tomo 69.

Interlude. *Las Ynstrucciones del Virey*
1. AGN Tomo 67.
2. Marshall.
3. W. Cook, Illustration 27.
4. Thurman.
5. AGN Tomo 44.
6. Caamaño.

Chapter VII. *Las Goletas*
1. Novo y Colson.
2. Thurman.
3. AGN Tomo 397.
4. Unless stated otherwise, the account of Galiano's voyage is taken from the *Relación.*
5. Thurman.
6. Quoted in Marshall.
7. Marshall.

Interlude. *Oficiales y Tripulacion*
1. Herr.
2. Vaughan.
3. AHN, Madrid, Est. 4290.
4. Salva
5. Vaughan.
6. Sotos Serrano.
7. Wagner, 1933.
8. Novo y Colson.
9. Sotos Serrano.
10. Vaughan.

Chapter VIII. The Voyage to Nootka
1. Maurelle.

Interlude. Ozette
1. Makah.

Chapter IX. The Native People.
1. Wilson.
2. AGN Tomo 277.
3. Walker.
4. AGN Tomo 69.
5. Chief Ambrose Maquinna, in conversation with author.
6. As quoted in *Relación*.
7. Wike.
8. Beaglehole, p. 320.
9. Fleurieu.
10. In: Sound Heritage.
11. Bodega, 1792.
12. Wilson.
13. AGN Tomo 65.
14. Beaglehole, p. 323.
15. Bartroli.
16. Bodega, 1792.
17. Bodega, 1792.
18. Turner and Efrat.

Interlude. The Fur Trade
1. Howay, 1973.
2. Beaglehole, p. 326.
3. Bodega, 1792.
4. Fisher.
5. Haswell.
6. Boit.
7. Fisher.
8. *Relación*.
9. Quoted in *Relación*.
10. Wike.
11. Novo y Colson.
12. AGN Tomo 69.
13. Wike.

Chapter X. The Strait of Juan de Fuca
1. AGN Tomo 70.
2. AGN Tomo 67.
3. AGN Tomo 67.
4. Wagner, 1933. Original source not found.
5. Wagner, 1933.

Interlude. Eighteenth Century Navigation
1. Berton.
2. AHN, Madrid, Est. 4290. In fact, the chronometer Arnold 176 was put aboard later, so the statement is not strictly true.
3. Enciclopedia General del Mar.
4. Author's observation.
5. AGN Tomo 558.
6. *Relación*, 1805 edition.

Chapter XI. The Gulf of Georgia
1. Marshall.
2. Wagner, 1931.
3. AGN *Provincias Internas*, Tomo 134.
4. AGN *Provincias Internas*, Tomo 134.
5. Walbran, under "Savary."

Interlude. Place Names
1. AGN Tomo 68.
2. In: Sound Heritage.

Chapter XII. The Narrow Waters
1. The Spanish account, which is followed here, sometimes confuses Broughton with Johnstone, another officer.
2. AGN Tomo 68. The instructions were from the Viceroy to Bodega y Quadra. Presumably they were passed on to Galiano.

Interlude. Quadra at Nootka
1. Bodega, 1792. Unless otherwise stated material in this section comes from this source.
2. AHN, Madrid, 4290.
3. AGN Tomo 70.
4. AGN Tomo 70.
5. Wike.
6. AGN Tomo 70, also Riobó.

Chapter XIII. The Commissioners
1. Bodega, 1792.
2. W. Cook, p. 366.
3. AGN Tomo 67.
4. AGN Tomo 70.
5. B.C. Provincial Archives, 1913 Report. Letter to Bodega y Quadra from Robert Gray.
6. In: B.C. Provincial Archives.
7. In: Marshall.
8. Bodega, 1792.

Chapter XIV. Nootka Abandoned
1. AGN Tomo 67.
2. W. Cook, p. 397.
3. AGN Tomo 70.
4. Bodega, 1792.
5. Bodega, 1792.
6. Herr.
7. Quoted in W. Cook, p. 403.
8. Jones.
9. AGN Tomo 71.
10. Walbran, under "Kendrick."

Appendix. Vocabulary of the Nootka Language.

The vocabulary of the Indians of Nootka Sound was recorded by a number of eighteenth-century visitors. James Cook made a brief word list in 1778. Joseph Ingraham, who was mate of Robert Gray's ship in 1789, gave a word list to Martinez, which the latter translated correctly into Spanish. It appears that this was the starting point for the list in Moziño's *Noticias de Nootka,* although there are differences. Bodega y Quadra included a word list which differs slightly from that of Moziño whose vocabulary appears in several different documents. The version given below is taken from the edition printed in Mexico in 1913.

The vocabulary appears in two parts. The main list of words is in the manuscript used by the editors of the 1913 publication. A supplementary list is in an introduction written by Alberto Carreño. It consists of words which are not contained in the manuscript used by the editors in 1913 but which are found in other documents, principally in the 1802 publication of the *Relación* of the Galiano voyage. The two lists are kept separate in this Appendix, and the original alphabetical order in Spanish has been retained.

The eighteenth-century Spanish spelling has not been modernized; the letter "V" is used instead of "U" at the beginning of a word and similarly "Y" is used for "I." The English translations are by the author. When there is more than one possible meaning for a Spanish word, that which is most probable at Nootka has been selected. Moziño included the following note in his manuscript:

> This language lacks the letters *r, ñ,* and *l.* The natives have some difficulty in pronouncing the words they learned from us; on the other hand, aspirates abound (in their language) of which I have written the strongest as *G* or *J* and the softest as *H.* The *sh* is pronounced as in English, and the *X* as *cs.*

The Spanish called both the people and their language "Nootka." This is not correct. The people are the Mowachaht and following English practice the language could be called "Mowachan." The word "Nootka" has been retained because it appears so often in the Spanish manuscripts, with various spellings.

The main list from the *Noticias* is as follows:

Spanish	Nootka	English
	A	
Abajo	Vs-te-el	down
Abrazar	Ap-qui-xitl	to embrace
Abuelo	Coa-uteh[1]	grandfather
Azeyte	Ha-ca-mitz	oil
Acostarse	Tac-petl	to go to bed
Agua	Cha-ac	water
Aguila	Agua-tene	eagle
Ahora	Tla	now
Ayer	A-meo-i	yesterday
Ayre	Yue	air

Spanish	Nootka	English
Alas	Tlabas-pa-ato	wings
Alcahuete	Copa-za	intermediary
Almagre	Coatzma	red ochre
Alma	Cua-ja-mitz	spirit
Almoada	Achuco-imi-me	pillow
Alto(a)	Sa-ya-cha	high, tall
Amanecer	Vp-cus-taa	dawn (n. or v.)
Amarillo	Hitz-tzuc	yellow
Amigo	Hua-cas	friend
Andar	Yac-tzuc	to walk
Ano	Ait-zatz	anus
Año	Jachicinic-shitle	year
Anular (dedo)	O-at-zo	ring finger
Aprender	Amiti-ami-ta	to learn
Aquel	Tlautla	that
Arca	Toco-nec	chest (coffer)
Arbol	Sut-chazt	tree
Arcoiris	Muz-ta-ti	rainbow
Ardilla	Cha-tu-miz	squirrel
Arenque	Cluz-nitz	herring
Arena	Muc-cu-metz	sand
Arriva	Yltz-pe	up, above
Arrojar	Huaj-chilt	to throw
Avalorios	Ato-jui	beads
Azul	Tup-cuc	blue

B

Spanish	Nootka	English
Ballena	Ma-ac	whale
Barba	Apac-tzutl	moustache (? beard)
Bajo(a)	Ana-chas	low
Beber	Nac tzitl	to drink
Besar	Tzi mec-ti	to kiss
Beso	Temesti-xitle	kiss (n.)
Blanco(a)	Atit-tezutl	white
Boca	Yetla-tzutl	mouth
Borracho	Tutz-yutz	drunk
Bostezar	Ax-ect-zitl	to yawn
Brazo	Ca-ya-pta	arm (n.)

C

Spanish	Nootka	English
Cabello	Api-si-up	hair
Caveza	Tag-chite	head
Caliente	Tlug-mas	hot
Calor	Tlupa	heat
Canaletes	U-jua-pe	paddles
Canoa	Cha-patz	canoe
Cargar	Ap-cuitz	to load

Spanish	Nootka	English
Casa	Ma-ja-ti	house
Casa sola	Hui-coac	single house
Ceniza	Tlin-tenes	ashes
Cama	Chimi-elg	bed
Cancion	Nuc	song
Cantar	Nu-nuc	to sing
Carne	Chis-qui-mis	meat
Carrillos	Ka-a-mas	cheeks
Cejas	Acac-si-chi	eyebrows
Cendal	Na-much-mop	? barb of feather
Cerca	A-nas	close to
Chico(a)	Atl-ma-chis	child
Ciego	Maco-ulg	blind, blind person
Cielo	Naz	Sky
Cinco	Sut-cha	five
Clavicular	Natlah-caz-te	collarbone
Cobre	Chi-puz	copper
Cojo	Quitj-zac-tle	cripple
Cola	Naa-cha	tail
Comer	A-uco	to eat
Como	Co-co-coa	like (adj.)
Compañeros	Hu-u-mitz	companions
Conducto auditivo	Cuachime-hime	? earhole
Corazon	Tug-tu-ja	heart
Coronilla	Apet-zatcue	crown of head
Corpulento(a)	Yg-e-pit	fat (adj.)
Corrientes	Teza-ac	currents
Cortar el cabello	Chi-que-mejutl	to cut the hair
Cortar el Vello	Tlaco-mejutl	to deflower
Costillas	Natlag-caz-te	ribs
Cubrirse	O-cu-chas	to put on a hat
Cuello	E-me-u-titl	neck
Cuerpo	O-u-matle	torso
Cuero de zorro	Co-yac-tzac	fox skin
Cuervo grande	Coog-xi-ne	raven
Cuervo pequeno	Ca-e-ne	crow

D

Spanish	Nootka	English
Dar	Cana-je	to give
Dar bofetadas	Flos-me-jutl	to pummel
Dar puñadas	Tliqui-tzu-jutl	to punch
Decir	Si-sani	to speak, say
Decir de memoria	Chanec-tzitz	to recite
Decrepito(a)	Yg-cheme	feeble
Dedos	Ve-tza	fingers
Degollar	Cat-que-shitle	to cut a throat
Delgado	Tzi-ti-yu	thin

151

Spanish	Nootka	English
Derramar	Tzi-chitl	to spill
Dia del verano	Yac-nas	summer day
Dia del ynvierno	Nitz-nas	winter day
Dia	Nas-chitl	day
Dies	Ha-yo	ten
Dios	Coa-utz	God
Dispertar (?despertar)	Asg-xitl	to awaken
Dolor	Meya-li	sorrow
Doncella	Otiquit	small fish
Dormir	Huci-che	to sleep
Dos	Atla	two

E

Spanish	Nootka	English
Enano	Nagua-zitl	dwarf
Encarnado	Hi-yuc	red
Enojado	Huic-gei	angry
Enfermo	Ta-elt	sick
Entender	Ca-ma-tas	to understand
Entrar	Yni-itle	to enter
Erigirse el pene	Tluc-tze-ma-ja	to have an erection
Erutar	Ninitetz-ca	to belch
Escapulas	Tla-tza-pe	shoulder blades
Esclavina	Cli-ti-ni-qui	cape
Escroviculo	Yg-ni-yutl	? thorax
Escupir	Tapa-tzitl	to spit
Espalda	Ynapatl	back (n.)
Espinilla	A-ama-nutl	shin
Espinazo	Co-o-nes	spine
Espirea	Tzi-quipi	spiraea
Esperesarse	Tag-yactl	to stretch (oneself)
Esperarse	Hui-na-pe	to be hopeful
Estar dispierto	Peni-ca	to be awake
Estar callado	Yma-ja	to be silent
Estar atado	Mamatl-ape	to be worthless
Estar suelto	Tlica-patl	to be fluent
Estar bueno	Chimi-ta	to be well
Estar en pie	Tlequilh	to be standing
Estera	Tle-xatl	matting
Estomago	Tat-cha	stomach
Estornudar	Toupex-chitl	to sneeze
Estrellas	Taa-tuz	stars
Escretar	Yzt-map	to defecate

F

Spanish	Nootka	English
Flecha	Si-jati	arrow
Flor	Coi-matz	flower
Fluxo del mar	Ja-yutl	flood tide
Fornicar	Hua-huata	to fornicate

Spanish	Nootka	English
Frente	Ap-pe-a	forehead
Frio	Ate-quitz-majas	cold?
Frio(a)	Magtl-as	cold?
Fruto	Pat-ai-hua	a fruit
Fruto en gral	Chamas	fruit (collective)
Fuego	Enic	fire

G

Garganta	Yni-yutl	throat
Gaviota	Co-ne	seagull
Gemelos	Coa-yas	twins
Gibo	Yeh-jumil	hunchback
Gorrion	Quil-chup	sparrow
Grande	Asco	big
Granizo	Cat-tzumen	hail (n.)
Gritar	Aja-mi-yu	to shout
Grueso(a)	Huic-xac	thick
Gustar	Cha-mas-patl	to taste
Gustame	Ojo-tic	I like

H

Hablar vno solo	Tla-nac	to talk (one person)
Hablar mucho	Ny-tlac	to talk (many)
Hablar de secreto	Tluitl	to talk secretly
Hacer	Ma-muc	to make
Hacer gestos	Chis-tzitl	to gesticulate
Herir	Chi-chi-nic-etl	to injure
Herirse	Chi-althas	to be hurt
Hermano	Catla-ti	brother
Hermana	Clutz-mup[2]	sister
Hierro	Chiqui-mi-ne	iron
Hijo	Tana	son
Hojas	Tla-tla catzeme	leaves
Hombre	Cha-cups	man
Hombre veraz	Tag-cotl	truthful man
Hombre embustero	Aaita-aita	liar
Hombre rico	Co-as	rich man
Hombre pobre	Hua-hua-pee	poor man
Hombre alegre	Ap-jec	happy man
Hombre disoluto	Chyz-aets-coatz	dissolute man
Hombros	Ha-ha-pimitl	shoulders
Hoy	Tup-shitl	today
Hoyuelos de cara	A-a-mas	? cheeks[3]
Humo	Ysh-cuitz	smoke

Y

Y(conjuncion)	Huai	and
Yerno	Co-ec-zo	son-in-law

Spanish	Nootka	English
Yelo	Coug	ice
Yerba	Mucu-metz	grass
Yndice (dedo)	Coyoeh-jac	index finger
Ynfierno	Pina-pula	hell
Yo	Sia	I
Yris	Chami-ehtl	rainbow[4]

J

Joven	Ahui-jleti	youth
Jugar o canzear	Ami-chap	to joke

L

Labios	Chipitl-esma	lips
Ladron	Capit-zitle	thief
Laguna	A-oc	lagoon
Lastimar el humo	Coti-tza	To hurt the pride[5]
Lavarse las manos	Tzau-tze nic	to wash one's hands
Leche	Clitz-zit	milk
Lengua	Chup	tongue
Lebantar	Tzo-cuitl	to lift
Labarse[6]	Tle-qui-sit	to get up
Lejos	Sa-ya	far off
Lobo marino	Cocoa-quitra	seal (animal)
Loquios	Tzahuatz-que	afterbirth
Luego luego	Zu-shi-nic	immediately
Luna	Ata-jas	moon

LL

Llama	Ysh-cuitz	swamp
Llamar pr. señas	Tlutl-tlutl-nu	to signal
Lleno(a)	Ca-ma	full of
Llevar	Yni-ta-pe	to carry
Llorar	Ei-jat	to weep
Llover	Mitz-zitle	to rain
Lluvia	Mic-tla	rain (n.)

M

Madre	V-mec-zo	mother
Mañana	Amic-tla	morning, tomorrow
Manco	Coa-coat-zo	one-armed
Mandivulas	Tzi-huap	jaws
Mano	Cu-cumit-zu	hand
Mar	Tup-pel	sea
Mar bonancible	Aupac	calm sea
Matar	Tzoc-tzitle	to kill
Matarse a si mismo	Tzuc-tzitle	to commit suicide
Manzana	Mu-mu-octl	apple
Mear (hombre)	Oc-tzitl	to urinate (man)

Spanish	Nootka	English
Mear (muger)	Omec-tzitl	to urinate (woman)
Mecerse	Pual-lato	to shake oneself, to be mixed
Medio	Ta-yec	middle
Medio dia	Apeh guene-nas	midday
Medio (en)	Ape-hu-ne	half
Mentira	Ai-tlajatl	a lie
Mentiroso	Aita-aita	liar
Meñique(dedo)	Caol-ca	little finger
Miembro viril	Qui-mis	penis
Mio(a)	Na-na-nichi	mine
Mirar	Nape	to look at
Mira aquello	Tzu-map	look at that
Mocos	Ante-mitz	nasal mucus
Mojarra(pez)	Chz-apa	perch (fish)
Montaña	Nuc-chi	mountain
Muchacho	Ta-nas	small boy
Muchos	Ayi-mil	many
Mudo	Muco-itl	mute
Muger	Cluz-ma	woman
Muger joven	Ag-coatl	girl
Muger hermosa	Tlul-cul-ma	pretty woman
Muger fea	Pisul-cluz-ma	ugly woman
Murallas	Tehit-tema	external walls
Muslos	Apezuh-tatehi	thighs

N

Spanish	Nootka	English
Nalgas	Y-tla-tle	buttocks
Nariz	Nit-za	nose
Navio	Mamatle	ship
Negro	Tzuc-mitz	black
Niña	Clut-tzas	female child
Niño	Maetl-catzis	male child
Nieto	Coi-utch	grandson
Nieve	Coitz	snow
No	Huic	no
No Señor	Huicque	no sir
No ves	Chita	? can you not see
No comer	Nisi-meje	? not to eat
No tener que comer	Quina-jac	To have no food
Noche	Ata-jai	night
Noche de verano	Nitz-atajai[7]	summer night
Noche de Ynvo	Yac-atajai	winter night
Nordeste (viento)	Achi-lit	northwest wind
Norte (viento)	Yu-ilx	north wind
Nosotros	V-jaac	we, ourselves
Nubes	Silg-huasa-mis	clouds

Spanish	Nootka	English
Nube del ojo	Mumuc-se-me	cataract (eye)
Nuca	Yndeniat-zatz	nape of neck
Nuera	Co-et-zo	daughter-in-law
Nueve	Tzahua-cuatl	nine
Nuevo(a)	Chu-selg	new
Nutria de mar	Co-cotl	sea otter

O

Spanish	Nootka	English
Ocho	Ati-cuatl	eight
Ojos	Caah-si	eyes
Oir	Na-a	to hear
Olas	Cuaug-cuag	waves
Oler	Mitz-mitza	to smell
Ombligo	Aime-ne	navel
Orbita del Ojo	Oahtl-oahtl	eyeball
Orejas	Pa-pe	ears
Orina	Oe-xitl	urine
Oso	Chi-mitz	bear (animal)

P

Spanish	Nootka	English
Padre	Nu-huc-zo	father
Paladar	Apeza-meza	palate
Pantorilla	Tanua	calf (leg)
Parir	Hei-ne-metl	to give birth
Parida	Tzaguas-coe	Note 8.
Pasearse	Juzt-jutza	to take a walk
Pato	Ma-ma-ti	duck
Pecho	Tlapez-ahuma	Chest (of a person)
Pechos de muger	Eni-ma	Woman's breasts
Pedazo de Palo	Za-hu-mitz	piece of stick
Peinarse	Tza-hu-mitz	to comb one's hair
Peine	Tza-chi-ca	comb (n.)
Perro	Ae-mitz	dog
Pestañas	Achag-psimg	eyelashes
Pescado	Sum-ma	fish in general
Pico de ave	Tlup-cu-maa	bird's bill
Pie	Tlus-ten	foot
Piedra	Muc-zi-e	stone
Piel	Tuh	pelt
Piel de Nutria	Coa-tlac	sea otter pelt
Piel de oso	Clic-jae	bearskin
Planta del pie	Apat-tzutl	sole of foot
Pluma en el ala	A-apsu-enotl	wing feather
Pluma arrancada	Atelag-tleg	plucked feather
Playa de Ycoatl	Tlaza-tzetle	beach at Ycoatl[9]
Playa del rio	Cuitz-pitz	beach at the river[10]
Poco(a)	Huitz-tzu	not much, little

Spanish	Nootka	English
Podre	Tza-camis	pus
Ponerse el sol	Op-a-apto	sunset
Porque	Guasi	because
Preñada	Tlitl-tzitl	pregnant
Prestar	Acol-tli	to lend
Primero	V-ac-tzatl	first
Puerta	Tam-xi	door
Pulgar (dedo)	Ehja-comitz	thumb
Pulpo (pez)	Til-sup	octopus

Q

Spanish	Nootka	English
Quadro(a)	Jaca-mitl	square
Quadriles	? Apezu-thtle	hips
Quando?	V-yi?	when?
Quatro	Nu	four
Quanto?	V-na?	how much?
Que?	Acac?	what?
Quebrar	Coat-chiti	to break
Quemadura	Mug-cho	burn (n.)
Quemarse el cabello	Aiz-qui-mi-yutl	to burn one's hair
Querer	A-ha-coe	to wish
Querer mucho	O-ca-yo	to long for
Quien?	Atzit-tza?	which?
Quijadas	Tzi-huap	jaws[11]

R

Spanish	Nootka	English
Rayo	Tug-ta	ray of light
Raiz	Muit-me-metz	root
Ramo	Tla-cai te-me	branch
Rapaz	Tanac-ac-etz	lad[12]
Rascarse	Mi-qui-nicoa	to scratch oneself
Rasgar	Tze-quies-hitl	to tear
Raton	Yps-co-ne	mouse
Refluxo	Piscep-chist	ebb tide
Regla de la muger	Ait-tzat-tzitl	menstruation
Reirse	Tli-joa	to laugh
Retozar	Miap	to frolic
Rincon	Ame-ni-quitl	corner (inside)
Rio	Tzac	river
Relampago	Tleg-chitl	lightning
Robar	Tzu-cuitl	to steal
Rodilla	Chag-tzi-te	knee
Romper	Cua-chitle	to break
Roncar	Op-ta	to roar, to snore
Rededor (al)	Tut-xitl	around
Redondo(a)	Yp-qui-milt	rounded
Recivir	Ca-a	to receive
Red	Gua-gua-miti	net[13]

Spanish	Nootka	English

S

Sacar la lengua	Chup-cep-tzitl	to stick out the tongue
Salir	Y-ne-as	to go out
Saliva	Tlatl-mez	saliva
Salmon (pez)	Tzu-ja	salmon
Sangre	Atzi-miz	blood
Sardina (pez)	Ami-multz	sardine[14]
Sed	Na-ca-me-ja	thirst
Seis	Nu-pu	six
Semen del hombre	Atl-xitl	semen
Semen de la muger	Hitl-tzitl	woman's "semen"
Sereno	V-pac	serene[15]
Sentarse	Tec-pitl	to sit down
Serrucho	Tehit-jac	hand-saw
Si	E-e	yes
Si Señor	Ee-o	yes sir
Siete	A-a-petzuntl	seven
Sobaco	Atli-pu	armpit
Sobrino	Hu-e-o	nephew
Sobrina	Atz-ec-zo	niece
Soñar	Pu-es-nac	to sound (drum, bell, etc)
Sorber	Chit-tzitl	to suck or sip
Sordo	V-pulg	deaf
Sol	V-pel	sun
Sombrero	Chia-puz	hat
Soplar	Pup-hitl	to blow (breath)
Solo	Tza-huit	alone
Subir	Sa-ac	to go up, raise
Sudor	Hup-ze-machitl	sweat (n.)
Suegro	Co-ec-zo	father-in-law
Suegra	Co-ec-zo cluzma	mother-in-law[16]
Suelo	Yz-te-il	soil, ground
Suyo(a)	Tlaut-tuz	his
Sur (viento)	Tuchi	south wind
Suspirar	Hitl-tzitl	to sigh

T

Tais del Ynfierno[17]	Yz-mitz	Satan
Tallo	Guchas-ate-me	stalk (of plant)
Tarde	Yac-tzuc	late (adj.) or afternoon (n.)
Tela de la capa	Atj-mop	woven fabric for cape
Tener	Vnac	to have (possess)
Tener sueño	Po-atla-to	to be sleepy
Tener sed	Naca-mejas	to be thirsty
Tener hambre	Ague-quetle	to be hungry

Spanish	Nootka	English
Tener mucho que comer	Acho-mishaca	to be ravenous
Tierra	Tzi-tzi-mitz	land
Tio	Na-ec-zo	uncle[18]
Tirar de la ropa	Cu-titz	to undress
Tirar del brazo	Tzu-tzuas	to lead by the arm
Tobillo	Ai-xi	ankle
Tocar	Tlug-tuj	to touch, play an instrument
Tomar	Ma-a	to take
Tocer	Huatzac-citl	to cough
Trabajar	Ma-muc	to work[19]
Tres	Catza	three
Trenza del cabello	Op-cat-at clema	braid (hair)
Tripas	Tzi-yup	guts
Tu	Sua	thou
Tullido	V-pe-mitl	paralytic
Tuerto	Pipe-zul	one-eyed
Tuyo(a)	Suat-zis	thine

V (includes U)

Spanish	Nootka	English
Vbula o campanilla	Cha-chi-yume	uvula
Ves?	Na-na-nichi?	dost thou see?
Verse en los ojos de otros	Nech-i-zu	to see oneself as others see one(!)
Venas	Tlacut-apte	veins
Venado	Mo-huech	deer[20]
Vegina de la Orina	Az-pa-tu	bladder
Vello del pubio[21]	Apach-chime	pubic hair
Vender	Ma-cuc	to sell[22]
Venir	Cho-co	to come
Ventana	No-as	window
Ventana de la nariz	Cu-cus-tlate	nostril
Verde	Tlitz-mitz	green
Viejo	Mig-tug	old
Vientre	Yc-tas-tlas	belly
Viento duro	Pisec-as-yue	strong wind
Viento bueno	Oco-maya	good wind[23]
Visco	A-ni-cha	cross-eyed
Vive fulano?	Ti-itch?	Is "so-and-so" alive?
Vltimo	Tlac-tzatl	last (adj.)
Vno	Sa-huac	one
Vñas	Chatl-techa	fingernails
Vomitar	Alh-alh-la	to vomit
Vtero	Tanat-zas	uterus
Vulva de la muger	Chig-lit	vulva

Spanish	Nootka	English

X

Xefe	Tais	chief

This is the end of the vocabulary printed in the 1913 edition of the *Noticias*. In the introduction, Carreño gives a supplementary list of words ascribed to Moziño which appear in the 1802 edition of the *Relación* of Galiano's voyage. The list follows:

A

Agua salada	Tupulthz	salt water
Agujero	Cajat-za	hole
Alegre	Ap-jei	happy
Aljaba	Si-hatat	quiver (arrows)
Almejas	Clochima	clams
Anoche	Amiathai	last night
Ansar	Mamati	goose
Anzuelo	Chimene	fish-hook
Aprisionar	Capehil	to imprison
Aqui	Aco	here
Arco	Muztatu	bow or arch
Aretes	Nima	ear-rings
Arpon	Sakijao	harpoon
Azotar	Clin-caca	to whip

B

Barba de ballena	Tsicomis	whalebone
Barrena	Suti-seto	drill (n.)
Bastante	Aquia-quis	enough
Biga[24]	Nipsilc	roofbeam
Bonancible	Au-pac	calm, moderate
Borrascoso	Piseq-chut	stormy
Bueno	Clush	good

C

Callar	Tza-mac	to keep quiet
Cambiar	Macuco[25]	to trade
Canoa de guerra	Tequinna	war canoe
Cara	Isslus	face
Cebolla	Eisak	onion
Cedro	Humis	cedar
Cierra	Musaap	?saw[26]
Cinta	Sistul	band, tape
Colgar	Matlaplez	to hang
Concha	Izto-co-ti	abalone shell
Cortadura	Chic-chinic	cut (n.)
Cortar	Chuchitl	to cut
Cosa tuya	Suat-tzis	thy thing[27]

Spanish	Nootka	English
Cosa de aquel	Tlaut-tzis	his
Cosa nueva	Chu-selg-xi	novelty
Cuchillo	Cuitzo	knife
Culebra	Haycyech	snake
Cuñado	Yu-mec-zo	brother-in-law
Cuñada	Chinap-zec-zo	sister-in-law
Cutis	Tug-coac	skin

D

Dame	Acoalthlay	give me
Dame que comer	Cah-cat-si	Give me food
Danza	Oyelthz	dance (n.)
Dedo pequeño[28]	Catlecac	little finger
Despedirse	Yut-sasemut	to say goodbye
Dientes	Chi-chi-chi	teeth
Dimelo	Ametechitl	tell it to me
Disparar flechas	Clie-chitle	to shoot arrows

E

Encender luz	Pajtlitz	to strike a light
Entendimiento	Tli-mas-tec-nec	understanding
Entiendo (no)	Aai-majas	I do not understand
Esclavo	Coulz	slave
Esconder	Cuilx	to hide
Escopeta o fusil	Pu	shotgun or musket
Escribir o pintar	Chis-shitl	to write or paint
Escucha	Ala	lookout, sentry

F

Flojo	Guic-toc	loose
Fresas	Callquintapa	wild strawberry

H

Hija	Clutzul	daughter
Hipo	Titicoseja	hiccough
Hombre viejo	Mutug-yacops	old man
Hueso	Ammut	bone

I

Intestinos	Tzi-yup[29]	intestines

L

Lanza	Suikaiak	spear
Larga	Tahetchitle	? long[30]
Ligero	Visisich	light (adj.)
Lodo	Chi-zimits	mud

M

Madera	Hiniose	wood
Malo	Pishec	bad

Spanish	Nootka	English
Morder	Machitle	to chew
Mosca	Mats cuainna	fly (insect)
Mujer vieja	Mituc-clutzma	old woman

N

Spanish	Nootka	English
Nadar	Sujsa	to swim

P

Spanish	Nootka	English
Palma de la mano	Upatsul	palm of the hand
Pavimento	Iz-te-itl	floor
Pelear	Huina	to fight
Pequeña	Pitthlab	small
Pesado	Coutjijich	heavy
Pescado colorado	Chahapa	red snapper
Pierna	Clishtlina	leg
Pinchar	Cuchitle	to prick
Pino	Kucuitlac	pine
Presto	Oyea	quick

Q

Spanish	Nootka	English
Quitatelo	Huanatultl	Get out!!

S

Spanish	Nootka	English
Silencio	Tsamah	silence
Sombra	Malzani	shadow
Sonarse	Sinisquishitle	to blow one's nose

T

Spanish	Nootka	English
Tabla	Zlo-oc	board, plank
Tejado	Tlu-uc	roof
Temor	Tujuc	fear
Templar	Citachil	to trim sails
Truenos	Tuta	thunder

V

Spanish	Nootka	English
Vertido	Cat-sac	? spilt
Vete	Henchel	Go away

Z

Spanish	Nootka	English
Zozobrar	Haxup	to capsize

Although Moziño gave the infinitive form to all the verbs in the vocabulary, he recognized that the corresponding Indian words represent various tenses and persons. He gave a partial conjugation of the verb *comer* (to eat) covering the following forms:

Spanish	Nootka	English
Aquel come	Auco[31]	someone eats
Aquellos comen	Auca	people eat
Yo comí	Aucmiz	I ate
Tu comiste	Auc	you ate (fam.)
Aquel comio	Aucmitiz	someone ate

Spanish	Nootka	English
Come tu	Aucce	eat (imperative)
No comi yo	Huicmutz	I did not eat
No comío aquel	Huicmutitz	someone did not eat

The vocabulary, with some duplication contains 535 words, made up of:

Nouns and pronouns	317
Verbs	136
Adjectives and adverbs	66
Prepositions & conjunctions	12
Other	4

Notes to the Vocabulary

1. The Nootka word for "grandfather" was interchanged with the word for "grandson." This has been corrected.

2. A transcription error has been corrected. The Nootka word for "Hermana" was omitted, reappearing as the word for "Humo."

3. Apparently a duplication. See *Carrillos.*

4. The entry under "Arco" in the supplementary list below suggests that this may be wrong, and the correct word is given under *Arcoiris.* It is possible that this entry means the iris of the eye.

5. In the manuscript the Spanish words are written as shown. In all probability this is an error, and it should have been written "lastimar el humor."

6. From other documents, it seems this should read "lebantarse."

7. This word has been interchanged with the following one, or else the words for a summer and winter day have been interchanged. *See* "Dia."

8. "Parida" is a noun, meaning one who has recently given birth. In modern Spanish it usually means an animal.

9. "Ycoatl" or "Yuquot" is the Indian name for the village called "Nootka" by James Cook.

10. It is not clear which river this means. There is no large stream near Yuquot.

11. A duplication of "mandivulas."

12. As an adjective, "rapaz" could mean "rapacious." On the slender evidence of the "Tana" root, the noun has been chosen.

13. An apparent mistake. A net is "tsima."

14. Species uncertain.

15. *See* mar bonancible.

16. Literally "woman father-in-law." *See* muger.

17. It is unlikely that "Hell" or its chief had any meaning for the Indians. Interestingly, Moziño used the Indian word "Tais" rather than the usual "El Principe" as the title of the Prince of Hell.

18. Family relationships gave Moziño some problems. "Na-ec-zo" means "grandfather" according to the present Hereditary Chief of the Mowachaht, Ambrose Maquinna.

19. Duplication of "Hacer."

20. Hence Mo-huech-aht or Mowachaht, the people of the deer.

21. *cf* Cortar el vello.

22. The same word is given by Moziño for "Hacer" and "Trabajar." *See* Note 19.

23. In fact this means "good weather." (Ambrose Maquinna)

24. "Biga" in modern Spanish means a chariot. It is more likely that this word is the modern "viga."

25. A ubiquitous word. *See* Vender, Trabajar, etc.

26. The modern "sierra." Other spellings, and meanings, are possible.

27. Duplication of "tuya."

28. Duplication of "meñique" in main list. The Indian word given here is supported by other lists.

29. Duplication of "tripas" in main list.

30. Both masculine and feminine forms are given for adjectives in other entries. There is a noun "larga," but it has no meaning which is plausible at Nootka.

31. This form used by Moziño as the infinitive.

Index